Edward T. Wright, Esq.

HOW TO USE COURTROOM DRAMA TO WIN CASES

PRENTICE-HALL, ENGLEWOOD CLIFFS, N.J. 07632

Prentice-Hall International, Inc., *London*
Prentice-Hall of Australia, Pty. Ltd., *Sydney*
Prentice-Hall Canada, Inc., *Toronto*
Prentice-Hall of India Private Ltd., *New Delhi*
Prentice-Hall of Japan, Inc., *Tokyo*
Prentice-Hall of Southeast Asia Pte. Ltd., *Singapore*
Editora Prentice-Hall do Brasil Ltda., *Rio de Janeiro*
Prentice-Hall Hispanoamericana, S.A., *Mexico*

© 1987 *by*

PRENTICE-HALL, INC.

Englewood Cliffs, N.J.

Library of Congress Catalog Card Number: 86-063757

ISBN 0-13-436080-X

Printed in the United States of America

This Book Is Dedicated
to My Wife
SUSAN REHR WRIGHT

Acknowledgment

One night my wife, Susan Rehr Wright, came home from a dress rehearsal at the Webster Groves Theatre Guild and suggested I enter a playwriting contest. This began a new life for me, spending part-time writing plays, and full-time adding dramatic techniques to a career in the courtroom.

I am grateful to her for this inspiration. I shall add it to those contributions she made as we crammed through my days at lawschool, struggled through the beginning years of a law practice, and joyously soaked up year after year of the challenges of a fascinating profession. When I sit back in my chair at my law office and look at the wall of photos of children and grandchildren, I say, "This is what happens when you invite a young lady to a college dance."

About the Author

Edward T. Wright has been a trial lawyer for more than thirty-five years, involved with nearly every kind of criminal and civil litigation. He fully qualifies for Melvin Belli's criterion that "a good trial lawyer is one who can walk into any courtroom, and try any kind of case."

One judge described him as "dramatic," but not "flamboyant." One editor referred to him as a "mild-mannered suburban attorney." His mild manner quickly disappears, however, in a heated cross-examination or during an emotional final argument to the jury.

He now practices law in Clearwater, Florida; formerly practiced in St. Louis County, Missouri; and is a member of the Illinois as well as Florida and Missouri bar associations. Soon after graduating from lawschool at Mercer University, in Macon, Georgia, he was elected a municipal judge, becoming the youngest judge in Missouri.

He is the author of several books, and his speeches and articles have appeared in more than forty journals and reviews. He was one of three judges appointed by the Missouri Supreme Court to draft rules of procedure for municipal courts.

He won the same playwriting contest that sent Tennessee Williams to Broadway, and for many years has been a student of drama in the theater. It is a blending of this dramatic background and trial experience that enabled him to write *How to Use Courtroom Drama to Win Cases*, which will help trial lawyers win lawsuits by using dramatic techniques in the courtroom.

Edward T. Wright, Attorney
Clearwater, Florida

What This Guide Will Do for You

Lower your voice at the right moment, move to a specific spot in the courtroom, ask an emotional question of a witness, and you can influence the jury and win your case. That's courtroom drama at its best.

It's no secret that if you play a case right in the courtroom you can alter the outcome that would be expected from just an impartial reading of the facts. Some attorneys have built their whole practice on repeating this phenomenon over and over again. You've seen those cases in which an attorney wins even with all the odds and evidence against him.

Now you too can discover the secrets behind the use of drama in the courtroom and improve your win ratio, increase the size of the verdicts you win, and your fees, and dramatically build your practice when the word gets around.

Here are the tips, techniques, and suggestions that the author has used successfully for more than thirty-five years as a trial lawyer involved in nearly every kind of criminal and civil litigation.

Concrete methods that will help you play your case right to the jury fill fourteen chapters with constant reminders of what to do at each turn to make a trial more dramatic and help you win your case.

Drama is the theme, the courtroom is your stage, and the judge and jury are the audience—and everything is related to staging the case through the use of drama and dramatic techniques to win over your audience.

Solid, how-to information takes you right from picking the theme, the goal you want to reach—the climax—at the very beginning, setting the stage by picking the jury, pacing the drama deliberately, from the opening statement, gradually unfolding the drama to the jury to keep them on your side, using the right words to build credibility, using demonstrative evidence to capture their imagination, using conflict constructively to keep jury attention, knowing where to end each segment of the case, timing recesses during points in trial that will have jurors thinking positively about your client, building carefully to the final five minutes when you sweep them into your camp with the closing statement.

The mystery and mystique of great trial lawyers is swept away as you too learn how to use drama effectively. Go to the courtroom before the trial begins to get a feel of where you want to stand when you address the jury, talk to a specific witness, or show a piece of evidence. Block out where you will be at each moment when you are speaking, and think of how you want to use your body and your voice; review what you want to convey to the jury. When the jury is becoming bored, change the pace and liven things up with an exciting witness or new and dramatic evidence. All of these aspects and more play a part in your courtroom drama, and this guide brings you example after example of winning use of drama.

Get the jury on your side, and keep them there. From the very first moment you face these twelve people, you want to move them to your client's corner. They are watching and waiting, daring you to convince them that your story is the right one. Your tools are, the way to stand, look, say things, move, present your evidence, question your witnesses. All of these details add up to the creative use of drama in the courtroom.

Drama is heightened in today's courtroom through the use of demonstrative evidence, video that brings to the courtroom witnesses who are too sick to appear, or perhaps who are no longer living, or other dramatic evidence, and in some states the use of television cameras exposes the entire drama to the public's view.

You can meet these new courtroom challenges and emerge the victor with your own brand of drama, developing methods and a style that suits you, your personality, your specific needs, and each individual case that you try.

Make things happen in the courtroom with drama that motivates a jury to decide in your favor.

Contents

CHAPTER ONE

Start at the End
of Your Drama

SELECT THE THEME OF YOUR DRAMA

Every good drama has a theme, and courtroom drama is no exception. From the time the client walks into your office, you must begin building your case, and you do that by advancing the theme. That is why it is important to determine the theme early and build on it throughout the trial.

The theme of your lawsuit is the "why you are going to win." You must thoroughly understand this theme, or you will never be able to convey your message to the jury. From the very beginning, think about the theme and prepare your case in terms of how that theme will win.

Reduce Your Drama's Theme to Simple Terms

The easiest way to accomplish this is to reduce your theme to simple terms. If a child runs out in front of a car and the car cannot stop and hits the child, your theme will depend on which side of the counsel table you are sitting. If you are retained by the defendant, this is the case "where the child ran out in front of the car." If you are retained by the plaintiff, this is the case "where the car was travelling too fast to avoid hitting the child."

You often will find the theme of your case in the jury instructions. That is why it is best to examine those instructions when retained—not the night before you submit them to the judge.

Just as often, you will discover your theme while talking to your husband or wife or friends about the case. If your husband or wife says, "Oh, that's the case where that big company cheated your client," that is how the jurors might best remember the case. If he or she says, "That's the case where your client, the landlord, was drunk," you had better prepare yourself for the other attorney's theme, and remember that this is the case "where this poor guy spent six months in the hospital because his landlord, your client, failed to use part of the rent to keep the property in good repair."

Use Final Argument to Make Your
Drama's Theme a Winning Theme

Everything you do in your courtroom drama advances the plot to the time when you will rise and give your final argument. By then, your theme has become very familiar to your "audience." Based on this theme and the evidence you have introduced to support it, the jury is ready to hear you explain why they should return a verdict in your favor.

Start your case by preparing your final argument. You have to know the last thing you are going to say before you turn the case over to the jury, so introduce the evidence and build the drama to that point. Once you reach the final argument, you will be ready to tell the jury in simple terms the logical and natural course they should now take.

EXAMPLE: GUIDING THE JURY TO RENDER
A PLEA OF INSANITY

Everyday people packed into the courtroom to stare at the young man sitting behind the attorney at the counsel table. Counsel could tell that the jury hated this young man, and by the second day of the trial counsel sensed that the jurors were not too happy about him either.

Twice during this trial, a veteran court reporter had to ask for a recess because she was holding back tears as she attempted to transcribe the testimony. The young man had taken the blunt side of a hatchet to a young girl who had refused his attention. There was testimony as to his unusual conduct and medical testimony as to his lack of mental capacity.

Counsel rose from the counsel table to begin his final argument.

"I'm not going to repeat all of the disgusting things you have heard about during this trial, but I am going to ask you to stop and review in your own mind all of the evidence of these perverted acts, and then I am going to ask you to pause and ask yourself *one* question, 'Is our society ready to accept this kind of conduct as being normal?' I should hope not.

"If this young man was born during the early days of Greece, he would have been taken out on the side of a mountain and been killed, not for what he did, but for what he is. He is a scrawny young man who has a mind that is all mixed up.

"There are people in this courtroom today who would like to take him out to the side of a mountain and kill him, but we cannot do that, not under our law, and not in our society. We are concerned about people, not just the unfortunate who do not have good bodies and good minds; we just thank God that we are not like those people.

"But, we are concerned about the rest of the people who live in the society that has among them an increasing number of such people. We are concerned about what happens to this young man, because we are concerned about the people he will live among if and when he ever returns to society.

"This trial is about to end, and you and I will return to our offices, our homes, and our families. Richard Mantini is not going home. Either he will go to a prison, or he will go to an institution for the criminally insane. He will not sleep in his own bed, eat at his own table, or walk the streets of his own neighborhood. He gave up that right when he did this terrible thing.

"But, it is not his future but the future of others that should be your main concern. By sending him to a place where he will get the help he needs, you will make sure that this will never happen again. Sending him to prison to become a hardened criminal will only increase the chance of this happening again, for that prison will return the kind of person you and I do not want living in our neighborhood, and . . . he will return from prison if that is where he is sent. In your verdict, you have an opportunity to show the genuine concern, that I know you have, for what all of us have been living with, here in this courtroom, this week."

There was, of course, but one thing the jury could do and they did it. Lawyers don't create these situations, but they play an important role in making sure society reasons at a time when all of us are quick to set aside reason and give way to frustration and anger.

What is important about this argument? It is the same thing that is important about every plea of insanity and every plea of entrapment that stresses what you should know about every trial— you must start at the end. In these two defenses, you must throw all other defenses to the wind, so you must know what your final argument is before you begin your case. In other cases, this is not as obvious, but it is as important.

Plan your final argument the way you plan the rest of your trial—far, far in advance. However, be ready to change your plan on a moment's notice. This applies to every part of your trial.

EXAMPLE: CHANGING PLANS UNEXPECTEDLY TO WIN THE JURY

Counsel was about to try a jury case in a court of limited jurisdiction, and the defendant's attorney was about an hour late. Finally, the judge put the prospective jurors in the jury box, he took the bench, and the people assumed their positions around the counsel table, waiting for the defendant's attorney to fill the vacant chair.

When the defendant's attorney arrived, the prospective jurors appeared to have become a bit impatient with him, and he hurriedly sat at the counsel table and started to open his briefcase.

The judge called the plaintiff's attorney. "Counsel, you may proceed with the voir dire."

Counsel rose from the counsel table, looked slowly around the jury box at all of the prospective jurors, then smiled, faced the judge, and said, "Your Honor, this entire jury panel is acceptable to the plaintiff."

The judge turned to the defendant's attorney, and said, "You may proceed." The attorney stopped rushing through his file, and stood and then pondered a moment, wondering whether or not to ask any questions. I believe it was to his disadvantage that he pro-

ceeded, because each question seemed like a further intrusion upon the jury's time.

Lesson: It appears that you should never waive voir dire, but that is exactly what was done here and it paid off. Why? There are rules trial lawyers must follow, but there are exceptions to every rule.

CONCLUSION

Start your drama at the very end. Prepare your final argument the day you are retained, and improve upon it as you proceed with pretrial and trial. Plan ahead, and be prepared to adjust your plans as you proceed with your courtroom drama. This is where drama in the courtroom differs from drama in the theater; the script keeps changing on you, and you have to be prepared for those changes.

HOW TO BUILD TO YOUR FINAL ARGUMENT

1. Structure the story so each word adds drama.
2. Let the jury know that you are leading to something important.
3. Save the final dramatic moment for the very last.

CONSTRUCT THE FINAL SCENE OF YOUR DRAMA

Take pride in organizing and presenting your courtroom drama as a master of your art. All of what you do will lead to that final scene and end with a final argument that is well constructed.

From *voir dire* through final argument, you must know where you are going and exactly how you are going to get there. You must stand back and look and see if you have organized your presentation and carried it out. Your courtroom drama is like a play in that it must have form that is planned with imagination. By starting at the end, you'll know exactly where you are going, and then you can plan how to get there.

**Organize the Final Argument
as the Highlight of Your Story**

The final argument must be well constructed. The jury must know where you are going so they can follow you and anticipate and understand what is to come next.

Some good trial lawyers review the evidence, witness by witness. Whether you use instructions, your opening statement, the pleadings, or any other approach, follow some storyline that will take your jurors from the beginning to the end of your story.

Plan from the beginning how you are going to build up to those closing minutes. Once you have set the stage for those final minutes, you can then end with drama.

EXAMPLE: USING THE SIMPLE FACTS
TO PRODUCE DRAMA

The only notes for the final argument were copies of the instructions. Counsel had underlined parts of the instructions he had wanted to read verbatim.

"His Honor has instructed you relative to the law in this case, and you have now heard all of the evidence. I now want to go over these instructions with you, so we can see how this evidence matches the law of the case.

"His Honor instructed you in Instruction 10 that your verdict *must* be for my client *if:* First, the officer intentionally struck my client *and* he thereby caused a contact with my client, which was offensive to him *and* such contact would be offensive to the sense of personal dignity of a reasonable person *or* the officer intentionally restrained my client against his will.

"Now, the officer admitted that he struck my client, and that he did it intentionally. Every witness who took that witness stand, for plaintiff and defendant, testified to that, so that cannot be an issue.

"Next, we must prove that the contact caused by the striking was offensive to the sense of personal dignity of a reasonable man. My client testified that it was offensive to him, and other witnesses described the offensive nature of the contact.

"Is it unreasonable to be offended when an officer of the law strikes you in the head several times in front of your family and neighbors. *Of course not!* There can be no question under the evidence of this case, and the law as given to you by his Honor, that under these parts of Instruction 10 your verdict can only be for my client.

"But there is more to Instruction 10. It provides that even if you did not find a striking and the offensive nature of the contact, you must find for my client *if* you believe the officer intentionally restrained him against his will. The officer testified that he kept my client from 'getting away,' but then admitted my client wasn't going anywhere. My client told you he wanted to go into his home; his wife testified he wanted to go into his home and tried to go into his home, but this officer would not let him. The next-door neighbor said the same thing, and not one witness they put on the witness stand denied that my client was being held against his will.

"From the evidence, and the law given to you in Instruction 10, your verdict will be for Plaintiff, my client, and then you will have the job of deciding how much in actual damages this man should receive. In Instruction 8, his Honor gave you the rule you must follow under the laws of our state, and let me read that to you: '. . . then you must award plaintiff such sum as you believe will fairly and justly compensate plaintiff for any damages you believe he sustained as a direct result of the occurrence mentioned in the evidence.'

"You have heard the evidence, you know how much importance we place in this country, on the right of a person not to be beaten up on by the very officers we taxpayers pay to protect us. You know how much value we place on *not* being injured and you know the kind of verdict this man is entitled to for the damages he sustained."

Following this dramatic presentation, counsel proceeded with the instruction relative to punitive damages, and used the instructions as an outline. That is what counsel needs to obtain a judgment, so they are the checklist of what was proven. Counsel stands before the jury with the holy writ in his hands; these are His Honor's words he is reading to them.

You cannot maintain momentum throughout your entire final argument. Use the first part to give a logical analysis of your case. In Figure 1-1 you will find a graphic example of how to build your case from voir dire *up to the final five minutes of your final argument.*

CONCLUSION

You have spent the entire trial telling the jury your story. Now that you have reached the final argument, the part of the drama the jury has been waiting for, don't disappoint the jurors. Organize your final argument, construct each part of it as a craftsman, and deliver it in a way that the jury will listen attentively.

ORGANIZE YOUR FINAL ARGUMENT

1. Review the evidence by telling what you have proven.
2. Explain how this ties into the instructions so "under the law and evidence" you are entitled to a verdict.
3. Build emotional appeal so the jury is ready for the "final five."
4. Use the final five minutes before the jury as though this is all the jurors will remember of the lawsuit.

BUILD UP TO THE FINAL FIVE

This is the moment that you and the jury have been waiting for! Even during the rest of the final argument, you have been laying the groundwork for this. Now, you have earned the right to stand before that jury and use the last five minutes before you send them off to the jury room to convince them of your cause.

Figure 1-1   The Narrowing of the Process of Persuasion

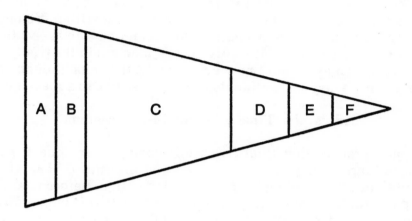

A   *VOIR DIRE*—Introduce your characters and cause.

B   *OPENING STATEMENT*—Start your process of persuasion as though it is your last chance to win, it may be.

C   *EVIDENCE*—Convince the jury of your cause, through your case in chief.

D   *FIRST PART OF FINAL ARGUMENT*—Give a logical and convincing summary of your case, ending with a dramatic appeal.

E   *REBUTAL*—Answer points raised by opposing counsel during the first part of your rebutal.

F   *THE FINAL FIVE*—Pack into the final five minutes of your final argument all the drama that motivates a verdict and could not have been sustained for a long period of time. Months of trial preparation and days of trial have led you to this dramatic moment.

Prepare the "Final Five" Months Before Trial

The final five minutes are what your lawsuit is all about, so everything you do from the day you are retained is one more step toward that very specific goal. Each sentence of the final five may come from a deposition, an interview of a witness, or from a chance remark a friend made while discussing the case with you at lunch.

You must repeat the theme that you have been preaching throughout the trial, but it must not be a mere repetition. You have to wrap it up with words, demonstrations, emotions, and everything that is special, because it is a very special moment in the trial. That final thought may be a bit new or it may be the same thought you have given the jury earlier, but it must be presented in a special way.

Adjust the "Final Five" on Rare Occasions

You may prepare that final five while coming home one evening after talking with your client, after visiting him or her at the hospital, or after reading a successful deposition. Before trial that last paragraph is ringing in your ears, because that is what you are building toward. However, during the trial, or even during opposing counsel's final argument, a thought may drop in your lap that prompts you to change that final five, so be prepared to do so.

Let's take a look at the last five minutes of a final argument in a medical malpractice case:

EXAMPLE: USING THE FINAL FIVE IN A MEDICAL MALPRACTICE CASE

"You may wonder why one attorney can stand before you and suggest one amount that your verdict should be and another attorney sincerely suggest that your verdict should be in a much larger amount. In this case, there are two reasons and they are both very personal to me.

"First, I have a great respect for the human body, it is the only thing in the world that is really ours, and when it is gone, we are gone, as far as life as we know it here on earth. I feel very strongly that no one has the right to touch your body, without your consent, except for very good reason.

"No one has the right to put you under so that you have no control over your body, and don't even know what is happening to your body, except for very good reason. No one has the right to cut your body open and poke around inside it, except for very good reason.

"Mrs. Johnston was subjected to all of this because this hospital and this doctor negligently left a clamp in her body, and I do not feel that is a very good reason.

"Secondly, I love life; I have enjoyed these first 62 years, and I hope I enjoy many more; but I'll tell you one thing, if I stood on the sixth floor of this building and knew that if I got into that elevator there is one chance out of 200 that I would die, I would walk down every step of this courthouse to the parking level.

"I don't like those odds. Mrs. Johnston didn't like those odds, but she had no choice, because this doctor and this hospital left a clamp in her body.

"Throughout this trial, I have felt that my client has been at a disadvantage, because she is suing a hospital and a doctor. Did you notice the testimony of Dr. Aremos, that he could not think of one way the doctor could have avoided this? He probably did not know that the doctor was going to testify in this trial and that the doctor would tell you two ways he could have avoided this—first, by counting the clamps, and second if he or either of the two hospital assistants had looked before placing the bowel down over the clamp.

"Dr. Aremos testified for the hospital and for the doctor. Did it occur to you during this testimony that my client is his patient? What in the world has happened to the doctor-patient relationship? I think it is time that we make it very clear that it is the Lena Johnstons of this world who are paying the medical bills and making the doctors wealthy.

"These lawyers have come into this courtroom and tried to nickel and dime you into giving my client less than she is entitled to in your verdict. When a patient goes to a hospital or a doctor, no one nickels and dimes them. They receive full compensation, and when they make a mistake they should pay the full price, just like anyone else.

"I feel that you should bring back a substantial verdict in this case, because this woman deserves it, and because that is the kind of verdict you can be proud of for the rest of your life."

How much of this final five was there the first day the client walked into the attorney's office? Every bit of it! You must take depositions to show that one doctor will protect another. You must have the doctors admit on deposition that the chance of survival from an unnecessary operation is one out of two hundred. You must substantiate your final five from the moment you go to work on the case, but the drama is there. Use it! The results can be dramatic.

A lawyer called a fellow attorney and said his aunt had been on the jury and she had told him that the last five minutes of the final argument raised the verdict from $25,000 to $50,000. The final five minutes of the final argument does make a difference.

EXAMPLE: PROVIDING DRAMA
IN THE FINAL FIVE MINUTES

Murray Sams, one of the best trial lawyers in the country, has a unique method of leading into his final five. He simply tells the jury, "I want you to pay close attention to what I am about to say, because this is the most important thing you will hear during this entire trial." This is a simple, yet effective method.

Morris Shenker, a famous criminal lawyer who represented Jimmy Hoffa and others, gave his final argument in a tax fraud case, and as he was about to close, you could tell from the way he paused that he was about to conclude. He took a step toward the jury, stopped, and said in a quiet and confidential manner, "Bring back a verdict you can live with for the rest of your life." He won an acquittal.

In an armed robbery case, counsel told the jury:

"We are all concerned about crime, and we all have a role to play in trying to reduce crime. The judge, the prosecutor, and I . . . the witnesses who come to court to testify, and you, as member of the jury. I think you have the most important role of any of us, because you decide which of the defendants go to prison and which do not go to prison.

"Believe me, that is important, because if we send a person back on the streets who should go to prison, we make a serious mistake, and if we send a person to prison who need not go to prison, or who should not go to prison, we make an even bigger mistake. When we do that we manufacture another criminal and send back to your neighborhood and mine another person who will always be a criminal, and who will always be a threat to our peace and security.

"This young man was never a criminal and need not ever be a criminal. He had not received as much as a traffic ticket before that hot summer night last summer when his mother sent him to the drugstore, and he ran into some old friends from school, and took a ride to cool off. The prosecutor tells you when he got into that car he knew the driver was going to stop next to this old man and the other young man was going to pull a revolver and rob the old man.

"I have been representing this young man for six months and I don't know that. I have talked with his mother and his friends, and they don't know that. I have talked with this young man time and time again, and he tells me like he told you, that he didn't know they were going to rob that old man. If you send this young man off to prison you will not only needlessly manufacture a criminal and send him back into a society that already has far too many criminals, you will be making a mockery of our entire judicial system, a mockery of the very constitution that separates us from those countries that just don't care about people.

"You will be telling this young man that all of the evidence that we have brought into this courtroom means nothing compared to the opinion of the man who is paid by the State to prosecute him. It is not only this man's future, but the very integrity of all we believe in that is being decided here today."

The jury brought back an acquittal, partly because of the very practical concern about manufacturing criminals needlessly, and because they do believe in our Constitution and how it protects a young man, whose entire life could have been ruined because warrants were issued against all in the car, not just those active in the robbery.

In a civil case an attorney changed that "final five" while listening to the attorney for the insurance company give his argument. It is best to have at least the last paragraph or two, well in mind months before trial, but as the attorney heard opposing counsel tell the jury to give this woman her property damage, but not one dime for her injuries, the attorney could not resist changing the conclusion to his argument.

"As I sat here at the counsel table, listening to this attorney who has been hired by this company to try their lawsuit, I heard him tell you to pay this woman for her property, but not one dime for her injuries. As I sat here, I tried to remember where I had heard that concept, then I suddenly remembered.

"Under the Civil Code of the People's Republic of China, and under the Civil Code of the Soviet Union, you can recover for damages to property, but not for injuries to people. This lawsuit is being tried in the United States of America, and we are concerned about people. We are concerned about the fact that this woman has doctor and hospital bills that have to be paid. We are concerned about the fact this woman had to lie in the hospital for several months and that she could not be with her family, and could not enjoy what you and I take for granted every day of our lives."

The jury was concerned!

CONCLUSION

Those five minutes of final argument do make a difference. They are not just a summary of what you have been saying and what you have been proving throughout the trial. It must a *dramatic* message, given in a way that everyone on they jury can appreciate. Drama does not mean loudness or even an appearance of being dramatic. It is that rare quality of combining reason and emotion that enables the jurors to grab onto and believe what he or she basically wants to believe.

End with a dramatic impact.

QUICK HINTS FOR COMBINING REASON AND EMOTION TO GAIN DRAMATIC IMPACT

1. In the most emotional appeal, let the jury know the logic of our argument.
2. Use argument based upon reason, with words that prompt emotion.
3. Present reason with drama, and you will inspire an emotional response.

CHAPTER TWO

Select the "Audience" That Will Help You Win Your Case

GET FRIENDLY JURORS ACCEPTED—
AND UNFRIENDLY ONES EXCUSED

The trial starts when you rise to begin your *voir dire*. This is your first opportunity to unfold your trial strategy, and your first opportunity to begin "winning" your case. When you represent the plaintiff in a civil action, you are entitled to "meet" the prospective jurors first, and it is an "unforgivable sin" to turn that panel over to opposing counsel, without first having established a close relationship with these people who are going to decide your case.

No playwright would wait for the second act to begin his drama. No trial lawyer should "skip through" *voir dire* as though the drama had not begun. *Show them an exhibit*, or *tell them something that will catch their attention*, or *do something that will get their attention*. The opening scene of a drama must be dramatic!

By *voir dire*, you have decided such questions as whether the case will be tried before a judge or jury, and whether it will be tried in a state or federal court. In the venue that you have chosen (or inherited), you must select (or nonselect) your audience. That "audience" is anxiously awaiting the presentation of your courtroom drama. Don't disappoint them! Begin your trial with drama!

Don't Underestimate the Value of *Voir Dire* as Part of Your Trial Strategy

The greatest trial lawyers have always placed tremendous emphasis on a successful *voir dire*. Clarence Darrow once left a murder trial in California, took a train to Chicago where he selected the jury in another murder trial, and then returned to California.

First impressions are extremely important, in life and in the courtroom. Prospective jurors will form an opinion of you by the end of the *voir dire*. Make sure it is a *good* one. Since this is the only time during the trial that they can participate, don't deny them this privilege. *Make them a part of your voir dire.*

Listen to their answers. Make sure those answers do not speak out for a follow-up question that you fail to give. Let them know that you are interested in what they are saying. Include the entire panel in the discussion, even when you are talking to a particular juror.

Quickly Establish a Mood That Will Help Your Client

Jurors anxiously, and sometimes nervously, await the opening of the courtroom drama. They do not know whether it will be a comedy or a tragedy. They do not know whether they will be called upon to send someone to prison or to determine who is to pay for a human tragedy. It is to your advantage to establish a mood that best suits your client's cause.

If one attorney establishes a light mood, it may be difficult for the other attorney to change that mood to a more serious one. Mood determines how much money a jury will award, whether or not they will deal harshly with a criminal defendant, and whether they will decide the case with a technical strictness or will be very liberal in their treatment of the evidence and the law.

EXAMPLE: ESTABLISHING MOOD IN ONE SENTENCE OF VOIR DIRE

"At the end of this trial, if you agree with our experts that Mrs. Jones' husband would have lived another year if this doctor had performed his duties properly, will you then be able to place a dollar value on that one year of a human being's life?"

In one sentence, you have introduced three characters of your drama—the widow sitting at the counsel table, the man who is no longer living, and the doctor, who obviously did something wrong. You have also created the mood, you have told them that this is serious business, and that we had better be considering this as a big case. Also, you have probably set a courtroom record, by getting the prospective jurors involved in the discussion at the very outset.

Alternate Strategy: You may want to let the prospective jurors get settled down and relaxed a bit before you go to work. There are a few questions you can ask that will accomplish this very purpose.

However, if you are going to do this, direct those questions to the satisfaction of that purpose. Remember, if you create your mood immediately and they have more to consider than just normal nervousness of walking into the courtroom for the first time, they may appreciate even more your attempts to set them at ease after you have created your mood and introduced a few characters.

A few suggestions to set them at ease are: "This is the best part of the trial, since it is the only time you get to say anything"; "Just sit back and relax, and feel free to join in the discussion"; "Feel free to volunteer any information you think we might want to know"; "No lawyer is going to ask the panel a question that would be embarrassing"; "When I say, 'Have you been involved in a lawsuit,' I don't mean a divorce matter"; and, "If you don't understand a question, or feel you really can't answer it with a 'yes' or 'no,' just wave your hand at me, and we will talk about it."

"We will talk about it," may be the most important words you use on voir dire. That little tail at the end of a sentence may cause a prospective juror to open up and talk. You must constantly make the prospective juror aware of the fact you want him or her to discuss these matters informally, and even encourage them to enjoy this discussion. People are anxious to give you their views on just about everything in their own environment. Let them do so in your environment.

Start the Telling of Your Story during *Voir Dire*

Questions often are answers. Through questions, you can tell your story. *Examples:* "Would you have a problem returning a verdict of a million dollars if the evidence justified such a verdict?" "Do you have strong feelings on the subject of drunken driving?" "This lawsuit involves an occurrence that took place last New Year's Eve, in front of the Fox Theater, in which this man ran into my client with a truck as she was crossing the street; do any of you know anything about this incident?"

"Do you think a doctor should be held accountable for his negligence?" suggests a doctor was negligent. Why else would the lawyer ask the question? "Do you or any member of your family have a financial interest in, or are you or any member of your family employed by State Farm Insurance Company?" suggests that there is insurance in the case. Courts have devoted considerable time requiring plaintiffs' lawyers to couch the words properly and not overemphasize the question, in a vain attempt to keep the obvious from becoming too obvious.

If you represent the plaintiff, you can "go first" on *voir dire*, and if you fail to take advantage of this great opportunity, the advantage then goes to opposing counsel. If he fails to take advantage of it, you "go first" on opening statement, and have a chance to recover your fumble. However, if you don't start your drama on *voir dire* and opposing counsel *does* take advantage of your "kindness," by opening statement you are fighting to regain the advantage you surrendered.

STRATEGY DECISION: If you want a person to *stay* on the jury, should you ever suggest that this person be excused? My personal belief is that if you know a person will be excused for cause and you don't do it, opposing counsel undoubtedly will. You may be much better off being the *good* guy and making it possible for her to be excused.

EXAMPLE: EXCUSING A JUROR

"Mrs. Smith, I know it would be difficult for you to serve, after what you have been through, but if you did serve, you would follow your oath and be fair to both sides, wouldn't you?" Such a question is much more to your advantage than ignoring the problem and waiting for opposing counsel to say. "Mrs. Smith, I appreciate what you have gone through, since you lost a child and this lawsuit involves the death of a child, and I understand it is only normal that you have such strong feelings on this subject that there is just no way you could look at this impartially. Do you feel that for this reason, you should be excused from this jury and serve, instead, on a case that did not involve this issue?"

What To Do If the Judge Conducts *Voir Dire*

If the judge says, "You may begin *voir dire*," you had better take the ball and run with it. *Participate!* If your case is being tried in a courtroom in which the judge conducts the *voir dire*, participate to the fullest extent possible.

Where the judge conducts the *voir dire*, your participation often is most effective by submitting questions to the judge. In a case involving Scientologists, questions pertaining to every facet of the cult were submitted to the federal judge, and the thoroughness of the *voir dire* was proof that counsel had done extensive investigation and research to come up with such questions.

In a civil rights case, questions such as "Which organizations do you belong to?" and "Is any member of your family or close friend a police officer?" are fundamentally required. Every question that you would ask is a question that can be submitted to the judge to ask.

One outstanding trial lawyer told an ATLA convention that he keeps out of the federal court for one reason: he wants to conduct his own *voir dire*. A few federal judges have decided to give *voir dire* back to the lawyers. One way to keep, or regain, the privilege of conducting *voir dire*, is to conduct *voir dire* effectively, and this can be done with drama.

How to Recognize "Leaders" on the Jury Panel

There is one person on that jury panel who can win or lose your case for you. That is the potential foreman or forewoman, and you had better give this person your utmost attention. You must first establish who the leaders are, and then try to determine if they are for you, or against you.

Leaders are easy to identify. First, their position is extremely important. A person who holds a position of leadership or respect in daily life is a natural for foreperson of the jury. Second, the appearance of the person is important. Large people, scholarly looking people, friendly people all seem to attract other jurors to them. Next, look for someone whose experience relates to the matter being tried. If the case involves real estate, a person experienced in real estate is assumed to be a good person to guide the jury during its deliberation. Finally, watch how much he or she participates during the *voir dire*, and the reaction of the other members of the panel during that participation. You often can practically hear the other jurors express admiration or respect for a member of the panel who is playing a leading role.

Once you have spotted a leader, analyze him or her. He may be carrying another five or six jurors in his or her pocket, since about that many people on a twelve-person jury "go along" with what is being proposed, and the foreman or forewoman will do a lot of proposing.

EXAMPLE: SELECTING A JURY LEADER

The entire question for the jury was whether the electrical work done by the defendent caused a fire. One juror had been an electrician for twenty-five years and he was a large, good-looking person with a friendly smile. During the voir dire, *he participated vigorously and other members of the panel noticed him, and seemed to admire him. He was an obvious choice as foreman, if he remained on the panel. This is when you have a heart-to-heart talk with your client. "Are you positive about the soundness of the cause of the fire?" Learn what you can of the expertise involved, and listen to what the expert says. You decide to go with him. Your defense can stand the scrutiny of an expert on the jury. Members of the panel later tell you that you made the right decision! You are home free. You found someone to carry your cause to the jury room.*

ALTERNATE STRATEGY: Some good trial lawyers never leave an expert on the jury. You chose a jury to avoid one-man rule; why give up those other people and let one man decide? Who ever claimed trial strategy was an exact science? Know the two schools of thought, and apply the right one in the right case.

The trial lawyer had better know how completely delightful, or how completely devastating, the foreperson of the jury can be.

Have a Purpose for Each Question— Ask Only the Questions You Need

Each question you ask can obtain information about prospective jurors. The voir dire process is far more, however, than the gathering of information. Every question must either (1) create a mood, (2) establish credibility, (3) start telling the story, or (4) introduce characters of your drama. Know the purpose of each question, and make sure each question has a purpose.

EXAMPLES: *"We will be talking about a wall falling onto a man and crushing his body" creates a mood. "My client here at the counsel table is Reverend Smith; do any of you know him?" establishes credibility. "This case involves a story that appeared on the front page of the defendant's newspaper which accused my client of a crime he did not commit" begins the telling of your story. "Our expert witness in this case will be Dr. John Brown, the heart specialist from Harvard University Medical School; do any of you know of Dr. Brown?" introduces us to a character who will play an important role in your courtroom drama.*

Observe the Impact that Jurors Have on Each Other

During *voir dire*, all prospective jurors hear every question asked to every prospective juror and the answers to those questions. Sometimes two jurors come from the same neighborhood, work at the same office, or have something in common, and two votes may end up as one. Make sure the *dominant* of the pair is on your side. Make sure you give the others on the panel the opportunity to discuss what you are discussing with a particular juror. Merely turn and ask, "Has anyone else on the panel had a similar experience?" If one member of the panel is having an adverse impact on the others, shut him or her up, and if possible get him or her out of the courtroom, before the others are affected. When you are "telling your story," do it to the entire panel, or tell part to each of several members of the panel, but don't repeat the same story several times to several members of the panel.

Draw Out Juror Prejudices
as You Explain Key Concepts

Every lawyer has his or her own way of covering the presumption of innocence issue during *voir dire*. You might try an approach something like this:

"We all have our own ideas as to what the law should be and if we were senators we would probably introduce bills to change certain laws now on the books. During this trial, however, everyone in this courtroom is bound by the law in effect at this time. If you serve on this jury, you will take an oath to follow these laws, including the provisions in our state and federal constitutions. Do any of you see any problem in giving such an oath?

"One of the provisions of our state and the federal constitution is that this man sitting behind me at the counsel table is presumed to be innocent. Would any of you have any problem following His Honor's instruction to that effect?

"By this, we agree then that the fact an officer arrested him, and a prosecutor is prosecuting him, does not mean he is guilty—in fact, that is not even evidence of guilt . . ."

Suppose a man should rise from his chair and say, "Listen, buddy, if that kid wasn't guilty, the officer never would have arrested him?"

The proper response, of course, is: "Mr. Jones, you seem to have very strong feelings on this subject."

"Yes. I sure do."

"I guess those strong feelings would make it impossible to follow an instruction that *presumed* this young man to be innocent."

"Yes. That's right."

"Your Honor, I suggest that Mr. Jones be excused from jury service in this trial."

"Mr. Jones, you are excused."

ALTERNATE STRATEGY: This man should be gotten out of the courtroom as soon as possible, and before his philosophy taints the approach of other prospective jurors. However, many good trial lawyers would keep this man center stage, and use him to smoke out others who share his philosophy. That is what makes trial strategy a fascinating challenge. There is no single right way, but there are several *wrong* ways.

One wrong way is to be naive and not recognize there are others who feel the same way. In fact, jurors simply do not believe in the presumption of innocence. If this prospective juror is "drummed out" of the courtroom too hastily, especially with the judge ordering his dismissal, others who feel as he does may be reluctant to volunteer their philosophy. People often want to stay on the jury, and hesitate to get involved in the kind of discussion that has just resulted in the expulsion of a fellow member of the panel.

Consider turning to the panel and saying, "It is not at all unusual nowadays for people to feel the way Mr. Schmidt feels. Especially, with crime as it is, do any of you feel that way?" You are more likely to get a response, though you run the risk of Mr. Schmidt's philosophy becoming "accepted" by the jury. Remember, you *do* want to know the worst, because the worst is going to come out during the jury's deliberation.

CONCLUSION

Many lawsuits are won or lost during *voir dire*. In fact, many lawsuits are settled after *voir dire*. You can use this part of your drama effectively if you question with a purpose and really participate in the first exposure to the jury of you and your lawsuit. Selecting the jury is more than choosing who will, or will not, serve on the jury.

Voir dire is the beginning of the telling of your lawsuit. It is where the mood is set, and where your characters are first introduced. It is the beginning of the trial, from which all else must spring.

KNOW THE "AUDIENCE" FOR YOUR DRAMA

Those who work in the theater *know the audience*, and those of us in trial work owe our clients nothing less. Always try to play to the *best* "audience," for the *best* trial result.

Different Strategies for Trying Your Case

Where there is a choice, it is better to have a case tried by a jury. Judges often become "professional jurors," and the trial lawyer simply cannot let *one* person decide a case, especially if that one person has preconceived attitudes. The right to trial by jury is a precious one, and one that should be waived *only* if you're convinced that your client's chances will be better before a judge.

When a judge is to try the case, the lawyer's judgment of his outlook is particularly valuable, and that is why the client is paying him. Knowing judges in general, and judges in particular, is an important part of advocacy. If you don't know the judge's attitude on important issues, you had better find out.

Your personal experience is, of course, valuable for finding out about judges' attitudes; but your experience can be compounded many times by the experience of others. Lawyers are proud of their mass of information, and even opposing counsel will tell you things about the judge that you want to know. Be careful about stereotypes. Sometimes a judge who was very liberal when young, has become more conservative with age. How many criminal defense lawyers of the past are now handing out severe sentences, including the death penalty?

Pretrial conferences and other informal conferences with the judge tell you how he is going to rule and how he is going to "come across" to the jury. Motions in limine require the judge to "go on record" as to his attitude, where an informal indication does not suffice.

Don't avoid judges who are strict. They demand more of you, but they usually know what they are doing, so your client's cause may require you to look to other aspects of how that judge will handle the case. *Make demands upon yourself, and you will care less about demands placed upon you by the judge.*

A nonjury trial can be less formal, including the clothes you wear, the schedule you follow, and the manner in which you present your case. A possible relaxation of the rules of evidence can be very harmful, however, and it takes a real effort for some judges to ignore evidence they are not to consider. With the jury you get a fresh approach, where a judge has heard similar cases before, and has pre-conceived ideas.

Group Attitudes—and What to Do About Them

We have inherited a host of attitudes about particular groupings, a few made famous by Clarence Darrow. He wanted specific ethnic groups on his juries, whom he felt were more responsive to an emotional appeal and had warmer feelings toward his clients.

Putting people into groups is all right for "openers," but if that is where you end your inquiry, you will be in serious trouble. In a personal injury case, the plaintiff's counsel knew the juror was of a specific background and that he owned his own business. This would not qualify him as a plaintiff's juror under most concepts, but counsel liked the man and wanted to keep him on the jury.

After a substantial verdict was returned, counsel was very happy about the verdict, but this juror felt differently. He said, "I would have stayed there all week if I thought we could get more money for that lady." The woman was suing a businessman and the juror was a businessman, but he was also an individual who had his own thoughts on how much a human being is entitled to for personal injuries. The old stereotype in this case was wrong.

The old concept of keeping poor people on the jury when you represent the plaintiff has come under recent review. These jurors may give you $10,000 when other jurors would be satisfied with $5,000, but often the sum of $100,000 looks like a very generous verdict to jurors who cannot think in those terms. Other jurors may deal with huge figures with the realization that they aren't really that huge.

One of the nations leading trial lawyers, Phil Corboy, paid $22,000 for a jury study that helped him obtain a settlement of $5,500,000. The study showed that well-educated blacks are not as enthusiastic about giving large verdicts as others. In one personal injury case, a well-educated black, surprisingly, had cast the only dissenting vote.

This information was valuable to this great trial lawyer, and should be important to all trial lawyers, since it is a departure from the old stereotype and reflects the kind of change with which a trial lawyer must keep current.

Your lawsuit may not justify expenditure of $22,000 for a jury survey, but you can look at the Corboy study, and the results of other such studies, and can read all that is being written today on this subject. You can also *ask* people what they would do if on the jury. The same exhibit in a law office may prompt a client who comes in on a will to ask, "I'll bet some poor person fell on that horrible hole in the carpeting" while another may say, "How much was your client drinking when she fell?" When a friend has served on a jury, ask how various people on the jury reacted to various incidents.

How to Make the Most of Jurors' Individual Outlooks

You must know your jurors as you are selecting them and after the trial begins. When a successful prosecutor from St. Louis prosecuted his first case in more affluent St. Louis County, he told the jury that under the law and evidence, it *had* to return a verdict of guilty. But his opposing counsel said privately, "He is going to have to learn that in the county you don't tell a jury it has to do anything. Once a person gathers a few thousand dollars for a down payment on a home, no one tells him he *has* to do anything."

The Importance of Knowing Your Judge

There is a feeling among trial lawyers that federal judges are extremely independent and should be considered in a different light than state judges. For the purpose of discussing knowing your audience, we should recognize the federal bench as a different audience, and most federal judges will appreciate that approach.

To take an extreme example, a federal judge in a tax fraud case, after hearing about the poor health of a client, once said, "Counsel, I wouldn't worry about that at all. The federal government has some of the best health centers in the world."

EXAMPLES: DEVELOPING KNOWLEDGE ABOUT YOUR JUDGES

Perhaps federal judges can be brought into focus best by relating an experience of many years ago. A judge's father and my father had worked in the shoe factories together as boys and I would see the judge from time to time while he was riding the circuit in rural Missouri. He became one of the finest federal judges we have ever had, and I was to appear before him on a case in which I was attorney for Plaintiff, and there were about three firms representing the defendant.

On a lengthy docket call, I had to be in the state court on another matter, and the other attorneys had my trial schedule and had agreed to answer for me. When I got back to my office, my secretary told me the judge had dismissed my case. I went to the courthouse immediately to protest, and the judge signed a memo reinstating the case. Would the judge have done that to me—and to about ten lawyers that morning—if he was still a state judge, and up for reelection next fall? Probably not.

A woman who had never been in trouble before was charged with embezzlement in the federal court. A quick survey showed that during the past year the judge before whom she was to appear had had four similar cases come before him, and in each case had sentenced the defendant to prison. So counsel, by refusing to waive a grand jury, got the case reassigned to another judge, one who listened, and considered the special circumstances that warranted placing the woman on probation.

Probation, of course, does not come automatically! It comes after some dedicated lawyering. This begins with a thorough knowledge of the client, and this process should end with the attorney becoming enthusiastic as to the need for probation, and the client becoming positive in attitude and able to convince the court, as well as presentence investigators, that probation is the proper remedy. Character witnesses, employment assurances, and conferences with the prosecutor come next.

This woman had never done anything wrong in her life, and for one stupid mistake she was about to go to prison. There were circumstances to consider, but some judges think like a computer and really don't listen to those circumstances. Prison would have been a traumatic experience for this woman, from which she would never have recovered. Probation was granted in this case, both because of the special circumstances, and because of the "audience" that was willing to listen.

A trial lawyer once heard a judge express his belief in the importance of a father taking his son camping. This bit of knowledge paid off handsomely a year later. At a hearing before that judge, the attorney approached the bench and said, "Your Honor, I think a few minutes in chambers may save about a day of testimony." This is an offer no judge can refuse. The attorneys soon settled in their chairs in chambers. The judge picked up the file and asked what this case was all about.

Armed with prior knowledge, the attorney said, "Judge, I represent a man who wants to take his son camping on weekends . . ." With that, he sat back, with an impish feeling of how he could do this to a fellow attorney, and listened as the judge lectured his opposing counsel on the importance of a father taking his son camping. The attorney could have talked about bowling, baseball, or any number of activities, but with this judge, he pushed this button, and instantaneously had the judge arguing his case.

FEE TIP: Know which judges allow larger fees than other udges! A young attorney insisted on changing judges in a divorce matter, hoping the legal fee the young attorney's client was to pay could be lowered. The opposition lawyer laughed (to himself of *course) all the way down the courtroom corridor, going from one courtroom to the other. He knew the new judge would allow him $500 more than the original judge, and that he did. There is nothing wrong with knowing which judges award higher fees, as long as your client's interest comes first. In this case, the young lawyer tried to avoid a strict judge, and it ended up costing his client an extra $500.*

CONCLUSION

How you present your case will depend upon the audience to which you are presenting it. A retired person may not be as anxious to get back from court as a busy executive who is losing money while being in court. A judge who has heard enough argument may suggest that he doesn't need additional argument. A highly educated jury may understand an economist testifying as an expert, and a less educated person may prefer a high school math teacher who can put the case to him in simple terms.

You may choose the audience that will hear your case, but often you have less choice in this than in knowing the audience that was chosen through many factors, including some input from you. Knowing the audience, and presenting the kind of drama that the audience is most likely to be receptive to, is an important part of a winning trial strategy.

GENERAL QUESTIONS TO HELP SELECT
AND UNDERSTAND THE JURORS

1. How do you feel about serving on the jury?
2. Do you know of anything in your personal experiences that will have an effect upon your deciding this case?
3. Did you enjoy serving on the jury last time?
4. Did you feel serving on the jury was a worthwhile experience?

   Such open-ended questions can prompt a discussion that will really tell you about the prospective juror.

INTERACT WITH YOUR AUDIENCE
TO BUILD A COMPELLING DRAMA

A good actor becomes a part of the audience. He erases any barrier between him and those with whom he wants to relate. Actors and lawyers must share their drama with their audience. To do that, they must *interact*.

Share the Dramatic Experience with Your Audience

If the court does not tie you to a podium, get "close" to prospective jurors when you talk to them. If you are tied to a podium, at least "feel" close to them by thinking that you are talking with the prospective jurors informally and that they are going to *respond* to you.

When talking to one juror, include the others, and know that they are listening and judging by your dialogue with one of them. Stop and turn to the others and say, "Have any of *you* had a similar experience?"

You must constantly *share* views with the panel, and you must have them *share* their views with you. The thought that you are *sharing* encourages a willingness to give information. Keeping your questions away from what they are hesitant to share keeps members of the panel in a mood to participate.

Listening to a radio program in which guests are interviewed makes excellent training for *voir dire*. If the questions prompt yes or no answers, there is nothing left to talk about, and the bored audience will be delighted that the interview had ended.

Avoid yes or no answers by *asking open-ended* questions. "Mrs. Jones, how do you feel about . . ." cannot be answered with a "yes" or "no." "Did you ever . . ." will. You ask yes or no answers when you want a *commitment*. You ask open-ended questions when you want a *discussion* that could reveal something important.

If there is a sensitive area that must be approached, prepare your prospective juror for the discussion. "Mr. Jones, I know this is not easy for you to talk about, but . . ." Or, "It is important to my client that we know how you feel about . . ."

Include Every Prospective Juror in
Every Part of the *Voir Dire*

If one person notices that another is *enjoying* the *voir dire*, that person is more apt to participate. If he sees another member of the panel acting withdrawn and hesitating about answering questions, he will prepare to be defensive. And by the time you get to him, he will not participate and will withhold information.

Prospective jurors can identify with one another, with counsel, and with parties to a lawsuit. You will want that identity later in the trial, so get it at the outset. How many times have you been bored by a movie or television program because you could not identify with the characters of the drama?

As you talk with each member of the panel individually, do not suggest to the others that they can now take a nap, because you will not get to them until later. While addressing questions to the entire panel, note "groups" of people who will be questioned on a particular subject.

EXAMPLE: *Suppose only juror 1 and juror 8 have had previous jury duty. Rather than discuss this while addressing the entire panel, save it for the person-to-person part of the* voir dire. *This is done for two reasons: First, the computer tends to rob us of part of this personal contact by telling us marital status, employer, number of years employed, and other such information. But you must ask your question the right way. If you ask "Where are you employed?" the judge will impatiently ask you if you can read, and if so, read the computer printout with which you have been furnished. You should ask, "Where did you work before joining J.C. Penney?" By saving discussion of prior jury duty to the individual questioning, you have something to talk about, and your person-to-person discussion will be more genuine.*

The second, and even more important reason for saving certain questions for the person-to-person discussion is that you will have an opportunity to "group" your questioning with other prospective jurors, and keep them from being bored. While discussing prior jury service with juror 1, turn to juror 8, and say, "Mr. Brown, I believe you also served on a jury. Was that a civil or criminal matter?"

Not only does juror 8 know he is included in the discussion, but juror 10 knows that he had better stay alert, because he may be asked a question out of order. By such means, you keep the entire panel involved in the voir dire *at all times. In states in which you inquire of only six members of the panel at a time, the same approach can be used with the obvious modification.*

Use Even Hostile Prospective Jurors to Help Your Cause

If your opponent comes from a large law firm—with 25 to 100 members—using the firm's letterhead can be a very speedy (and very dramatic) way to draw out jurors who are prejudiced or downright hostile. Instead of just saying, "Do you know John Smith, my opposing counsel?" you can follow up, "Do you know any of the members of the law firm that represents this corporation in this lawsuit?"

Such a *voir dire* might go something like this:

"I am going to ask if any of you know any of the members of the law firm representing the defendant. First, does anyone know John Jones?"

A woman raises her hand and says, "Oh, yes, John set up one of my trusts for me." A short dialogue might follow, and then:

"Does anyone know Jim Smith?"

Let's say the same woman waves her hand and says, "Oh, yes, Jim set up a few of my corporations for me."

This woman would immediately be spotted as a character of this part of the courtroom drama, and she would obviously be an antagonist (bad guy), and not a protagonist (good guy). It must then be decided what role she should play. If you decide to keep her "stage center," she can be a vehicle for interaction between you and members of the jury panel—for a while.

Such a prospective juror would probably be quite happy to accept this role, and within a few minutes every other member of the panel will probably have had about enough of her. By then they will have identified her with the law firm representing the defendant, and to some degree, with the defendant.

Turning Time to Your Advantage

Toward the end of the *voir dire*, the discussion will often lead to the subject of time, to make sure no member of the jury has commitments that will interfere with listening to evidence, without distraction. Let's say it has been explained Monday morning by counsel that the case probably will last three days. (It is important to give the panel some timeframe so they can relax, knowing about how long they will serve.)

To continue the above example, let's say the panel is asked, as usual, if anyone has a commitment that might interfere with serving on this jury. Let's say further that this woman's hand goes up, and she explains that she has a tea Thursday afternoon. It might be explained that the trial should end by then, but suppose counsel adds, "However, if there is an emergency of some kind, and we do not finish as planned, I am sure you would not let that tea interfere with your duties as a member of this jury, would you?"

The juror would undoubtedly give assurance that she is a good citizen and willing to sacrifice by being late, or even missing the tea, in order to participate in this important part of the democratic process. Counsel might then turn to another woman who has raised her hand.

"Yes, Mrs. Brown, on what afternoon do you have tea?"

The panel laughs and Mrs. Brown says, "Oh, no, it's just that I arranged for a babysitter through Thursday—will I have a problem?"

Counsel turns to the bench and says, "Mrs. Brown, the judge presiding over this trial has been a trial judge for many years, and was an outstanding trial lawyer before that. There is *no* way this judge is going to let us lawyers waste a lot of time, and there is no reason we should not be out of here by Wednesday night."

What has been accomplished thus far in the *voir dire*? Counsel has discovered a means of interacting with the members of the panel. He has divided the panel into those concerned about "being late for tea," and those concerned about "picking up kids." By interacting with the jury panel, counsel has identified with those who are going to serve, because, the woman at stage center should not serve. Once she has served a purpose, with one stroke of a ballpoint pen, she should be struck from the jury, and make her exit "stage right."

CONCLUSION

The *voir dire* can be fun, and you should *make* it fun. If you properly interact with the members of the panel and cause them to enjoy this experience, you will learn about them, you will build credibility for you and your cause, and you can begin to tell your story. By the end of the *voir dire*, you will have selected your audience, and you will have prepared your audience for the drama that is about to unfold.

The fact that many cases are "won," or settled, at the end of *voir dire* does not come by accident. It is the result of planning your *voir dire* long before trial begins, deciding upon the kind of judge or jury before who you will appear, choosing the members of your audience from the panel given you, understanding those who are in you "audience," and interacting with that audience from the moment you rise to begin your courtroom drama.

HOW TO PLAN YOUR *VOIR DIRE* PRIOR TO TRIAL
TO ENHANCE DRAMA

1. Use the *voir dire* section of your trial notebook prior to trial.
2. List general questions in this section of your notebook.
3. List questions that apply to this particular lawsuit.
4. Make sure the list of questions include problem areas, and areas that can help sell your story during *voir dire*.

CHAPTER THREE

Choose and Use Characters with Dramatic Impact

YOU ARE THE LEADING CHARACTER IN YOUR DRAMA

If you wanted to be modest about the role you are to play, you should not have become a trial lawyer. You must recognize your importance in the courtroom, not to satisfy your ego, but to advance your client's cause. You must frankly appraise your performance, as a good athlete would, but the most important part of your performance will be projecting to the jury as the kind of character they will like and will vote for in the jury room.

Try To Be the Kind of Person Jurors Like

You probably cannot walk into a courtroom and turn on an image that will impress the jury. There are such actors; but if a trial lawyer tries that, and the slightest insincerity slips through, the client's cause has been greatly damaged. It simply does not cost a dime to be a "good guy," and lawyers who realize this are apt to obtain better verdicts than those who do not.

The next time you meet a person for the first time, make a mental note of what you *like* and what you *don't* like about that person. This is precisely what the jury will do when they meet you and other characters of your drama.

Following a jury trial, a successful trial lawyer sent a questionnaire to each juror, and though the jurors insisted they were not influenced by the personalities of the attorneys, they did notice the differences. They were annoyed that one counsel was not prepared, and wasted time.

They considered whether or not one attorney was taking advantage of the other attorney, or of a witness. *IMPORTANT:* Each juror *expected* counsel to look out for his client! They thought it was "smart," "proper," and "right" that he did not help the other side.

Being a "good guy" can mean:

1. Looking like a good guy (dressing *properly* as one juror put it)
2. Showing respect for other people
3. Listening when others are talking
4. Smiling in a friendly manner
5. Being the kind of person others want to be around (start by asking if you are the kind of person you would want to be around)
6. Enjoying life and people
7. Caring (too many people today don't seem to *care* about anyone or anything)
8. Being yourself (don't pretend to be what you are not, and don't apologize for what you are)
9. Knowing how insignificant you are in the history of mankind, but how important all of us are to each other
10. Identifying with those with whom you are to interact

Those of us who enjoy life fully meet our daily challenges with a sense of humor. Some jurors have no sense of humor, no sense of caring, and no sense of responsibility. Your role in one lawsuit may demand a seriousness, and in another a playing down of the seriousness of the situation. *Know your jury* and *know your lawsuit*, and let the appropriate parts of your personality project.

If there is a cardinal rule to follow in the courtroom, it is that your should *be yourself*. You must feel comfortable about what you wear, where you stand, what you say, and what you do. That is because you are the leading character of your drama, and people will be looking at you. Much of a trial is not very exciting, but it's your job to make as much of it exciting as you can—and certainly to hold the jury's attention. You are center stage, so relax and enjoy the role, but remember the responsibility that goes with it.

A common view is that, if you feel opposing counsel is boring the jury to death, you may as well let him hang himself. However, this also presents an opportunity for you to come to the rescue and gain points with the jury. Make this your courtroom drama and don't let any of it drag. *Do something! Offer to stipulate! Waive certain requirements!* Interject *humor, questions, objections,* or at least *an observation.* Without giving up a strategic advantage, let the jury know that you are not going to let this important lawsuit put them to sleep!

Project the Right Image to the Jury

By realizing the importance of your role, you will be more likely to *project* your image to the jury. The most likeable character must get across to the audience what he is, what he is doing there, and why what he is saying is so important. All of this does not just happen; you have to make it happen.

If you are concerned about a prospective juror during *voir dire,* show that juror you are concerned. If you are touched by what a witness has just said, show the jury you are touched by it. But don't fake it, or the jury will see through it. Project yourself as the kind of warm human being the jury will accept.

Dale Carnegie influenced people for many years with books, speeches, and seminars, and one of his basic approaches was to appeal to "the noblest emotion." Emotion is a part of drama, but the kind of emotion you appeal to may tell the jury much about you. *You are a part of the emotion you bring into your courtroom drama.* If you project nobility, the jury will sense it.

Use Every Moment of the Trial
to Advance Your Client's Cause

There is no one particular moment during the trial at which to accomplish all of this. Every moment of the trial offers an opportunity. Use each moment to the extent that the moment offers that opportunity—no more and no less. Let each phase of the drama enjoy its dramatic moment to the fullest.

EXAMPLE: LEARNING TO MAKE EVERY
MOMENT IMPORTANT

A story is told about Everett Hulverson, one of the great trial lawyers of our nation, that in the course of the direct examination of his client, he once said:

"Now, Henry, you have told the jury about some of the injuries to you caused by this accident; now tell the jury about the injury inside your chest."

"I object, your Honor," his opponent said. "There is nothing in the pleading about an internal injury."

"Sure, there is, Judge," Hulverson replied.

The trial stopped for a moment while there was a quick review of the pleadings by judge and counsel. Everett then looked up and said, "I'm sorry, Judge, I was sure I pleaded that." Everett then turned to the witness and said, "Now, Henry, don't tell the jury about any internal injuries, since I didn't plead that, but tell them about your other injuries."

You couldn't tell if there were any internal injuries that amounted to anything, or if Everett had forgotten, but you could tell the jury was sure going to award some money for those internal injuries, because they just wouldn't want Everett to be embarrassed in front of his client.

Why did Everett get such large verdicts? What was his secret? I think it was because the jurors loved Everett. They just wanted to "give him the courthouse."

IMPORTANT! Few lawyers can ever acquire that rare quality that causes a jury to want to give them the courthouse. Don't become frustrated if you are not among the few who are so gifted. Learn what you can from these great trial lawyers, and look for the qualities that brought them such success.

Everett Hulverson had a down-to-earth warmness that made it easy for young lawyers to ask his advice on cases about to be tried. That is something they did not teach in law school; that great trial lawyers are usually gracious and helpful to beginning lawyers.

WARNING: Don't conclude that there are strategic advantages in not pleading important matters. Plead all that you can prove! If, however, you find you have failed to plead properly, remember how one great trial lawyer turned it to his advantage.

The leading character of any play is most effective when that role is blended with the other characters of the drama. Your role will help you win, if you remember:

> Don't announce the importance of your role; let the subtle suggestion reach the jury box by what you say, what you do, and how you do it.

Don't detract from your client's role, unless your client's role needs detracting from.

Do use your role to help bring life to the characters you introduce.

Don't let your role interfere with the telling of your story.

Do use your role to create an atmosphere and add drama to the telling of your story.

EXAMPLE I: *If you think a client would make a poor impression on the jury, you might arrange for him not even to be in the courtroom. Talk about "Mr. Jones," "this businessman," "the fellow being sued," "my client," and "the man who provides this service." The jury will look at you, dressed properly, showing them respect, as you use those terms to describe your client. And you'll be filling the void created by your client's absence.*

EXAMPLE II: *While representing a woman who has been injured in an accident, you should not only share the stage but should assume a very supporting role. Keep the client stage center, and use your role to add drama to the character she is projecting and the story she is telling.*

CONCLUSION

Some people simply do not like to live "stage center." The trial lawyer has no such choice, at least, during the trial of a lawsuit. There is not a moment during the trial in which some juror is not looking at him, and forming an opinion about him, which affects his client's cause. The only way to prepare for this is to *understand your role, to be what you want to project,* and then to *project what you are.*

CHOOSE YOUR CAST WITH CAUTION

Fate will deal you a cast of characters for your courtroom drama. It is up to you to decide which of these characters you will use, and how you will use them. It also is up to you to decide what additional characters you will add.

Use Your Good Characters at a Time and in a Way That Gives Dramatic Impact

When you are in the theater, you wait for the star to appear, and you applaud. In the courtroom, there is no grand entrance, but the timing of the entrance of your characters is very important. *Don't feel you are obliged to follow any order of appearance, based on custom.*

If you call your expert who is going to tell the story of damages, the jury will not be ready for him if it still has some question as to liability. If you call your witness who is going to touch on the subject of wealth of the defendant in a punitive damage case, and you have not yet convinced the jury that you are entitled to punitive damages, you have lost an opportunity for them to consider the extent to which punitive damages should apply.

The plaintiff need not be the first witness. You may want other witnesses to pave the way and prepare the jury for the plaintiff's testimony. Remember, your client begins to relate to the jury long before he or she testifies. Good characters should be a part of your courtroom scene before and after their appearance on the witness stand, depending upon how much exposure you feel is desirable.

If You Need Poor Characters in Your Drama, Use Them Carefully

Poor characters are those who make a poor impression and those who make no impression at all. If an accountant is going to bore the jury to death with a full day's testimony, you may consider stipulating as to his testimony. Boring exhibits are no great asset, yet they are better than boring witnesses. Don't use poor characters, unless they are necessary to your drama.

If a poor character is necessary to your case, plan how you will get his testimony before the jury as early as possible, and then get him off the witness stand, and *out of the courtroom.* The worst witnesses often are those who want to stay around and find out how the case is going. Don't let their shortcomings linger on in the courtroom. *Get them out!*

Prepare the jury for the poor characters of your drama. During the *voir dire*, you should ask, "Will you let your judgment be affected by the fact the only eyewitness to this accident has a criminal record?" During opening statement, on the other hand, you should tell the jury what you will prove, but not say with whom you are going to prove it. Just about the time you tell them that John Jones will testify as to such and such, old John may be out drunk and not show up in court. Absent witnesses are mysterious characters the jurors are likely to wonder about, and they can play a very damaging role in your drama.

Add Characters Only If They Improve Your Drama

The fewer witnesses you use, the fewer mistakes you can make. If a witness adds something, gives strength to your drama, and is a low-risk witness, use him. If not, you are assuming a risk you need not assume—even if the only risk is that of boring the jury. Prove your case and do it dramatically, but remember that you don't need a cast of thousands to accomplish that. CAUTION: Don't put a single witness on the stand for the sole reason that your client wants him to testify, or that your client has reimbursed the man a day's pay to be in court.

EXAMPLE: USING WITNESSES TO THEIR BEST ADVANTAGE

It is unusual to begin a trial with opposing party's deposition, but discovery offers unusual opportunities that can be used with devastating effectiveness. When you have such an opportunity, here is how to use it.

The opening statements have concluded, the jury is anxiously awaiting the beginning of the trial, the judge turns to you and says, "Counsel, you may call your first witness."

"Your Honor, I would like to read into evidence from page 7, line 13, of the Defendant's deposition."

"You may do so."

"'Question. Mr. Jones, did you admit at the scene of the accident that you had gone through the red light?'"

"'Answer. Yes.'"

"'Did you not also tell the officer that you had been drinking intoxicating beverages immediately prior to the accident?'"

"'Yes.'"

"'And you had consumed at least ten martinis within an hour or so immediately before the accident?'"

"'Yes.'"

If you have a deposition that can win your lawsuit during the first few minutes of the lawsuit, USE IT!

Why not start with the antagonist, the bad guy of your drama? Why not use him to erase from the jury's mind, once and for all, the question of how the accident happened, and to emphasize that alcohol may have been an important factor?

Make the Best Use of Your Characters

In court you must make the best of the characters you have been given, and their acceptablility to the judge or jury often will depend upon the manner in which you portray them. While waiting for his response to the prosecutor's final argument, one defense counsel tried to picture his client as others would picture him. He then looked at the police officer in shining uniform, and decided to begin his final argument, like this:

"I wish very much that in this case, I represented the president of a bank, because if I did he would be wearing a business suit, his hands would be clean, and he would speak clearly, and you could tell that he is a very intelligent man.

"However, my client is *not* the president of a bank. He is a laborer who works with his hands, and so his hands are not clean because he cannot keep them clean; he wears no business suit because he has no business suit. He can't afford one and he doesn't need one, so he is wearing these old overalls that you see, and he cannot speak well and explain to you exactly what happened because he has no education.

"Yet, the wonderful thing about our system of government is that this man is entitled to the same rights and the same consideration as the president of a bank. I would like to have you review the testimony of my client and in doing so, to imagine that these words were coming from the president of a bank, that these words are not coming from a laborer, and give this testimony the weight that it deserves under our constitution. If you do so, I am sure you will find that his testimony was *just as good as* that of the police officer who is a trained officer and a trained witness and who makes an excellent appearance and did such a good job of testifying.

"Under our constitution the outcome of a case does not depend upon appearance or *who you are.* It depends on whether or not the prosecution can prove *beyond a reasonable doubt* that the defendant is guilty. For you to reach such a decision in this case you must ignore the testimony of this good, hardworking citizen, whose testimony is worth just as much as the testimony of any other person on the face of the earth."

The defendant was found not guilty.

CONCLUSION

Good trial lawyers succeed when they use their characters properly. You *do* have some control over which characters you use, and you do have some control over how those characters will help reveal your story. You will reach your jury through the human beings who walk into the courtroom for the purpose of telling your story.

HOW TO MAXIMIZE ANY WITNESS
TO DRAMATIZE YOUR STORY

1. Introduce your witness by referring to him in *voir dire*, opening statement, or through another witness, so the jury expects him or her to say something important.
2. Prepare the witness so he or she will feel comfortable, by reviewing the testimony and explaining how you will conduct the direct examination.
3. Conduct your direct examination as though are are telling a fascinating story.

HELP YOUR CLIENTS COME ACROSS AS THE
PROTAGONISTS (GOOD GUYS) OF YOUR DRAMA

Watching the "good guys" win is our reward for watching drama. In the theater, he or she is the protagonist, and in the courtroom he or she is some person, expected or unexpected, who determines the outcome of your lawsuit. Make your client the protagonist, if you can; and if not, you or someone you put on the witness stand must carry this burden.

Present Your Client in a Way
That the Jury Will WANT You to Win

You are not only selling a lawsuit, you are selling a real live, human being. The jury does not return a verdict for some abstract agency; it returns a verdict for the person sitting behind you at the counsel table. Regardless of what manner of man or woman walked into your office, that is the person who is identified with your case.

Present All Your Characters in the Best Possible Light

Make that person as good a person as you can before you reach the courtroom. Think of his or her appearance, speech, and attitude. Tell that client that thousands of dollars are riding on how the client looks and acts in the courtroom. You can't call casting and tell them to send you a new plaintiff; you just go with what you have.

When you don't have much to go with, try to lessen the degree to which the jury will associate their verdict and your client. Maybe the jury will like your client's mother, and give her the verdict by identifying with her when they want to forget your client. Maybe you can cause the jury to identify with you or with a cause. The jury often dislikes the defendant in a criminal case, but realizes that our constitution would not mean much if they sent him to prison on such flimsy evidence.

To Detract from Your Client's Shortcomings:

Do make his personal appearance the best possible.

Don't make his presence any more prominent than necessary. (Consider when he should be present, where he should sit, and what he should be doing.)

Do emphasize issues and testimony of others, that are more favorable to your cause.

Do emphasize the best of your client's testimony by choosing the time for introducing it and dramatizing it.

Do tell his story through your role and other evidence, as much as possible.

Do prepare him for his role.

Do make issues more important than personalities.

You and every witness you put on the stand will be identified with your lawsuit. That is why you simply don't put certain witnesses on the stand. That is why you insist that certain witnesses "clean up their act" before you put them on the stand.

REMEMBER: For several centuries, right up to the recent adoption of the Federal Rules of Evidence, the law identified each witness you put on the stand with your lawsuit. Even today, in most states, you cannot impeach your own witness. This dates back to the old system of justice where each side would choose a combatant to represent his or her cause, and that representative *was* your client and your cause. If the law has so blindly identified the worst of witnesses who "just happened to be at the scene of the accident" as your witness how can we expect jurors, not learned in the law, to assume less.

Minimize the Effect of the "Good Guys" on Their Side

All good guys do not sit on one side of the counsel table. They will have their protagonists, and you must prepare for them. Start with your *voir dire*, and use every moment of the trial to prepare the jury and lessen the impact of that opposing witness who will hurt you. She may be an expert witness, or she may be an eye witness, but it is your job during discovery to find her and your job during trial to handle her.

Prepare for their "good guys" who are not in the courtroom. In a murder trial, don't think for one moment that the victim is not right there as an important character of the drama. Handle him during *voir dire* and opening statement. Respect the fact he is not alive and cannot be there in person to testify, but disarm him of any special status. If he was a bastard in life, you cannot let death elevate him to sainthood.

Make All the "Good Guys" Appear to Be On Your Side

Don't hesitate to use their good guys to convince the jury of your cause. "Then you agree, Doctor, that if the surgeon had followed this procedure it would have made a difference." Cross-examination is a wonderful time to invite their "good guys" to join your cause, and it is more effective when *they* have called the witness.

Here is how to accomplish that:

> "Officer, you arrested my client upon the complaint of Mary Smith, is that not true?"
>
> "Yes."
>
> "She is the manager of the drive-in restaurant, is that right?"
>
> "Yes."
>
> "You did not see my client do anything, did you officer?"
>
> "No, he was just standing there."
>
> "Did Mary Smith tell you what she saw?"
>
> "Yes. She saw the Jones boy and the Brown boy fighting."
>
> "Did she tell you whether or not she saw my client do anything wrong?"
>
> "She said she did not see your client do anything."
>
> "Officer, did you hear Mary Smith shout, 'Arrest all of them!?'"
>
> "Yes."

What has counsel accomplished? First, he has won the criminal case through an adverse witness in the person of a uniformed police officer. Second, he has obtained valuable evidence for a civil suit against the restaurant. REMEMBER: There is no law against taking a "cheap deposition" of witnesses in a criminal trial, for use in a civil trial.

EXAMPLE: GIVING THE JURY SOMETHING TO CHEER FOR

The trial judge told counsel, at a pre-trial conference there was no way a jury would return a $50,000 verdict for his fee in a divorce case, because counsel was "suing his own client." What the trial *judge did not know was, counsel had no intention of making the former client an antagonist, but, in fact would use her as a protagonist.*

During voir dire and cross-examination, counsel treated the former client as his own witness, and during the case-in-chief, he called her as his own witness. Counsel was trying his own lawsuit, the wisdom of which became evident as he proceeded with the direct examination of his former client.

"Do you think that during the time you were trying to prevent your husband from getting a divorce that I did a good job in representing you, in keeping him from getting a divorce?"

"Yes, definitely."

"Once you decided you did want to obtain a divorce, do you think I did a good job in representing you then, in obtaining the divorce?"

"Yes. I do."

"What about the settlement you received. Did you think I did a good job in that respect?"

"Yes."

"Did you tell me your husband made it very clear you would never get one dime from the sale of the stock?"

"Yes. He said I shouldn't have any of that."

"Did I advise you that you should have some of that money?"

"Yes."

"Did you tell me there was no way I could obtain any of that money for you?"

"Yes."

"After several months of work, was I able to prove the value of his net worth?"

"Yes."

"Did they then agree to settle for $250,000?"

"Yes."

"Did I advise you at that time that, due to your years of marriage, and your contribution to the marriage, that you were entitled to some of that money?"

"Yes."

"Did I later obtain for you a settlement of $500,000?"

"Yes."

"Did your former husband tell you not to pay this fee?"

"Yes."

"And did you tell him that you had agreed to pay it, and you felt you should pay it?"

"Yes."

"Is your son now handling your affairs?"

"Yes."

"Did he tell you not to pay the fee?"

"Yes."

"Does he know anything of the work I did in this case?"

"No."

"Did you want to pay this fee the day of the divorce?"

"Yes."

"But, he wouldn't let you?"

"Yes."

"Your husband and son told you not to pay this fee, and that was two weeks before I obtained this half a million dollar settlement for you, is that not right?"

"Yes."

"Did you tell me to stop negotiations?"

"No."

"In fact, you told me to proceed and try to get this money for you?"

"Yes."

"Did your son refuse to get involved in this matter until the very end?"

"Yes."

"Let me show you what has been marked Plaintiff's exhibit 8—do you recognize this piece of paper?"

"Yes. It is a letter I wrote after the divorce."

"Will you read to the jury the last sentence?"

"Yes. It says, 'I will never be able to repay you for all you did for me as my attorney.'"

The jury found one way to repay him as they returned a verdict of $50,000 plus interest. The former client was never the antagonist in this courtroom drama. The antagonist was her son, sitting behind *her in the courtroom, causing it to appear to the jury, even during recess, that he was calling the shots, and the jury now knowing that he knew nothing of the work that was done and did not even agree to get involved until the $500,000 settlement was worked out. What seemed like an impossible verdict to obtain was very easily obtained once the characters of the drama were unravelled for the jury.*

CONCLUSION

An audience wants someone to cheer for, and if that someone is on the other side of the counsel table, you had better prepare for whatever form that someone takes. (Often you can build drama with an empty chair, where the victim would sit if he were alive, or where an injured person would be sitting as plaintiff, if she were able to sit up.) There are visible and invisible characters throughout a jury trial, and the more good ones you can get on your side, the stronger are your prospects for winning.

HOW TO SECURE THE VISIBLE AND INVISIBLE CHARACTERS FOR YOUR SIDE OF THE DRAMA

1. Investigate immediately and commit the occurrence witness to your side.
2. Obtain your expert witnesses early.
3. Look for characters who will not appear in court, but who can be referred to during trial ("Why were you going to your mother's home?").

BE READY TO CONFRONT THE ANTAGONISTS (BAD GUYS) OF YOUR DRAMA

The antagonist of drama is the villain we hiss, the bully we boo, or the witness who changes his testimony in the middle of the trial. You must be prepared not only for the bad guy of your drama, but for that part of a good guy's testimony that makes him appear to be a bad guy. Your witnesses, as well as those offered by opposing counsel, must be screened for vulnerable qualities or vulnerable testimony.

The best witness can become an antagonist when he changes his testimony or admits something he should have told you about before taking the stand. When this happens rehabilitate with as little attention as possible, but if necessary, use depositions and all else to salvage the response originally expected. Where possible, use a recess to rehabilitate before ending testimony of that witness. IMPORTANT: Recognize all deliverers of bad news as antagonists, whose effect must be dealt with effectively.

Anticipate Weak Parts of Testimony and Make Them Stronger

Ignoring problems will not cause them to go away. Start during the *voir dire* to prepare the jury for any weakness in your lawsuit. Failing to recognize this simple truth of trial work is a failure to use your characters properly. How you use your characters will determine the outcome of your courtroom drama.

People like to hiss and boo, just as they like to stand up and cheer. There is some kind of emotional outlet that satisfies an audience when they watch the bully get the short end of it. If that bad guy is on your side, try to lessen the blow, and even try to disassociate him from your lawsuit.

Some jurors look with suspect upon any person making a claim for personal injuries. Make it clear at the outset that your client is entitled to damages. Back injuries are specially suspect so don't start with a "my back hurts" approach, but with convincing evidence as to what the client cannot now do that he or she could do before the injury.

Most jurors look upon people charged with a crime with suspect, whether they will admit it, or not. You must humanize the defendant in a criminal trial by calling him by his first name, standing next to him, asking him to tell something very personal, or having someone tell something personal about him.

There is someone on that jury who will notice the fact that your client is a black, a teenager, a woman, a foreigner, an elderly person, a wealthy person, an uneducated person, a farmer, a city-slicker, a Northerner, a Southerner, or some person with whom that juror does not identify.

Try to establish other identities. Poor blacks and poor whites do have something in common—a lack of money. All jurors have an adversity to pain. They probably feel some loyalty to their country. Build on these identities. They can identify with your client and his or her cause.

Dramatize the Weak Points in the Other Side's Case

Start with the discovery. After every deposition, study your notes and then study the transcript to see if you were fortunate enough to strike oil by finding a bad guy on their side. Make a photocopy of that page, blow it up for the jury to see, or at least underscore it several times so you can identify the villain with those words and use them when they will have the most dramatic impact.

From the beginning, you prepare the jury for your weaknesses, but you also save their weakness for that dramatic impact. You might want to hint at what is to come, or you might want to hit them with it without notice. Each bit of evidence must be examined to see what strategy best suits its effectiveness.

When your expert witness, your investigator, or your discovery hands you an important piece of evidence, handle it carefully and use it dramatically. Hold it in your hands very gently, inspect it, turn it over several times, and decide exactly how you are going to use it. If you don't use it effectively, you simply did not deserve receiving it.

When you have a photo that is going to prove the other party a liar, you may want to wait until that witness takes the stand. Let that witness describe in great detail a condition that simply did not exist. Then present the photo to him and let him try to escape the truth.

"Does this photo fairly and accurately represent the condition of the automobile you were driving as it appeared immediately after the collision?"

"Yes."

"I call your attention to the left fender, is that as it appeared immediately after the collision?"

"Yes."

"I have no other questions, your Honor."

At this point, you may want to have the photo admitted into evidence and pass it among the jurors. You do *not* want to let the witness explain the photo. The jury can tell from the photo that the witness is lying under oath, and you will remind the jury of that in your closing argument.

Some of the most convincing photos I have seen were in the "good old" pre-no fault days of divorce litigation. They could blow an alimony claim right out of the courtroom, or better yet, keep a case from ever reaching the courtroom. In every kind of litigation, that piece of evidence that is dynamite in the courtroom is equally effective at the settlement table. You owe it to your client to use the evidence when it will best serve your client, even when that decision robs you of one of your most dramatic courtroom moments.

Most lawsuits are settled, so there is no disgrace in having to settle a lawsuit, especially if you get a decent settlement. Every lawsuit has a price tag that depends upon many factors, including the effect a "bad guy" or a devastating bit of evidence will have on one side or other. Recognize this factor and don't give up a settlement that is more than you can get in trial.

LEARNING WHEN TO SETTLE

EXAMPLE: *A young woman was driving home from the hospital after a six-month checkup. Her baby was due within three months. The traffic slowed up, so she slowed up and then came to a stop. All of the other cars stopped, but the car behind her kept coming at her at a high rate of speed. There was nothing she could do, and his car ran into the back of her car. She was thrown into the steering wheel and was taken to the hospital. Before the ambulance arrived, the man who hit her came up and said he was sorry he didn't stop, that he was a contractor and was busy calling his office from his telephone in his Cadillac.*

They settled the case!

Another young woman was pregnant and left her kids with a neighbor so her husband and she could take a trip on his motorcycle. They were going down an old country road when a farmer pulled out in front of them, and she fell off the motorcycle. She was scared, because they were travelling pretty fast.

The young woman and her husband agreed to settle the case!

The world loves mothers, and expectant mothers, but it loves them much better if they are on the way home from a doctor's office than when they are riding on the back of a motorcycle.

The defense could have prepared the jury for the contractor with a phone in his Cadillac who ran into a pregnant woman, and the plaintiff could have prepared the jury for the woman who left her kids at home and was flying through the countryside on the back of a motorcycle in a highly pregnant condition. There is no law against driving a Cadillac, even one with a telephone in it. There is no law against riding on the back of a motorcycle, even when you are pregnant. But, if you entirely ignore the importance of those little good guy/bad guy qualities, you will make a strategical error.

CONCLUSION

Give the jury an opportunity to feel reassured about the weaknesses of another human being. It may give them some reassurance about their own status in life. If that weakness is not on the other side, however, minimize the effect. When you do have the right side of a lawsuit, dramatize it! Not necessarily with a brass band, but with timing, and effect.

In cross examining a witness, you may want to save a piece of dynamite for the end. "By the way, Mr. Jones, you testified on direct examination you had never heard of a Winston Berry. Now, let me hand you what has been marked plaintiff's exhibit 31." Let him look at the letter and let the jury look at the witness. "Now, Mr. Jones, will you look at the jurors and tell them whether or not that letter to Winston Berry is in your handwriting?"

Sloppy mechanics? Objectionable? I challenge opposing counsel to object. the jury already suspects this evidence is damaging to opposing counsel's case—now they will be certain. I can then turn and say, "I'm sorry, your Honor. Mr. Jones, do you recognize this piece of paper?" "Yes." "What is it?" "A letter I wrote to Winston Berry." "Your Honor, I would like to introduce this exhibit into evidence."

WAYS TO DRAMATIZE WEAKNESSES

1. Talk about their weak characters, even if they don't testify;
2. If they do testify, crossexamine with drama;
3. Refer to their weaknesses to the extent that you feel the jury is receptive; and
4. Use demonstrative evidence that pictures their weaknesses.

EACH CHARACTER IN YOUR DRAMA
MUST HAVE A PURPOSE

There are many characters in a drama, but each character must be there for a purpose. The playwright doesn't waste his valuable stage-time with a character that does not do something. The trial lawyer must be even more cautious, because he has more to lose than time. By putting an unnecessary witness on the stand, he may lose his lawsuit.

Know the Purpose of Each Witness and Exhibit

A beginning lawyer is impressed by the number of witnesses he can put on the witness stand. More experienced lawyers, and jurors, are more impressed with quality than with quantity. The experienced trial lawyer knows each character of his drama must *say* something or *do* something, or you simply don't need him.

Clients are the worst offenders of the "buy them with witnesses" syndrome. They often ask their attorney to "use this witness" or "use that witness," and too often the lawyer gives in to this ill advice. Control your lawsuit and do it by controlling the cast of characters you use in your drama.

First make a list of what you want to prove. Attach to each item on that list the kind of evidence you need to establish each fact. Then assign each task to a witness or physical exhibit, so you know who will prove what.

Here is an example of such a list:

Proof	Witness
1. Agency	1. Defendant's interrogatory
2. Cause of accident	2. Plaintiff
	Defendant's deposition
	William Butler, eyewitness
3. Injuries	3. Plaintiff
	Plaintiff's husband
	Dr. Smith
	Dr. Luten
	Bill Marks, her boss at work

(Another witness saw the accident, but she was such a poor witness that she was not used.)

Use Only What You Need

Corroborate, of course, when it is to your advantage. But every time you put a witness on the stand or introduce an exhibit, assess the value of that evidence and compare that value with the possible risk. Only through such a cost-effectiveness study can you determine the effectiveness and danger of what you are about to do.

EXAMPLE: KNOWING WHEN A WITNESS IS UNNECESSARY

One attorney called a witness who had held an important position and probably did so to impress the jury with the fact the man had held this position. His opponent could find no other possible reason for using this witness, but did find, during recess, an interesting article in the newspaper "morgue" of news articles dating back many years. The cross-examination went like this:

"Mr. Jones, you held that position for several years, did you not?"
"Yes."
"Why did you leave that position?"
"A new administration came in."
"And you left with the old administration?"
"Yes."
"And that was the only reason you left?"
"Yes."
"Did you leave at exactly the same time as the other members of that administration?"
"I believe so."
"You believe so. Is it not true that you left six months before the others in that administration?"
"I don't remember the exact date."
"Let me refresh your memory. I am handing you what has been marked plaintiff's exhibit 12; is this not a newspaper article dated four months before the old administration failed to get reelected?"
"Yes. I guess it is."

"And does this article not say that you were forced out
of office, under fire, at that time?"

"Yes."

"And does that article not state that you were forced
to leave office because of a bribery scandal?"

"Yes."

That witness was not necessary!

*In case of police brutality, the police commissioner, who knew
nothing of what had happened, was not there, and offered no
evidence of any value, for some reason, was called as a witness.
Again, opposing counsel capitalized on it. The cross-examination of
this witness went something like this:*

"Prior to becoming a police commissioner, you served
as a police officer, did you not?"

"Yes."

"Is it not true that as a police officer you told the
Mayor and Board that there was no police brutality in that
department?"

"Yes."

"And did you not testify a few minutes ago that you
have never known of any brutality by any officer in that
department?"

"Yes."

"Is it not also true that while a police officer you
walked into the federal district court and plead guilty to
participating in the beating of a seventeen-year-old boy?"

"That was a long time ago. Why do you want to go into
that?"

That witness was not necessary!

*A doctor had offered all medical proof that was needed of an
injury. However, a woman from the hospital then appeared as a
witness, and brought with her a bundle of medical records. A few
pages of the records that agreed with what the doctor had testified
were introduced, though certainly they were not necessary. Then*

this whole bundle of records came to the attention of the jury. Plaintiff's counsel cross-examined as follows:

"Let me call your attention to this document, and I have marked it separately as Defendant's exhibit 1. Is this a part of this man's record?"

"Yes."

"Will you read to the jury the last sentence on the first page?"

"Yes. 'Mr. Jones told the ambulance driver he was not injured by the fall.'"

That exhibit was not necessary!

CONCLUSION

The characters of your drama will help you win your lawsuit. The good work of those characters, however, can be harmed by the testimony of one witness who need not have testified. Even if you do not suspect a witness will cause you harm, REMEMBER, there is risk involved every time you put a witness on the witness stand, and every time you introduce an exhibit. So use only what you need!

HOW TO DISCOVER PROBLEM WITNESSES

1. Do not leave the interviewing of witnesses to others.
2. Do not close your eyes to the weaknesses of your witnesses.
3. Ask your witnesses questions at interviews that you feel will be asked on cross-examination.
4. Observe the witness, because how he or she says something may be as important as what is being said.
5. Learn as much as possible about the person who will testify, not just what the witness knows about the lawsuit.
6. Be alert as to testimony that is "too good."
7. Ask you client and others about the witnesses you are going to present to the jury.

INCLUDE ALL OF THE CHARACTERS
IN YOUR DRAMA

Regardless of how well you plan your case, the character who will win or lose your lawsuit may be one who does not appear to be a star of your drama. The jury is influenced by all characters, and often by those who seem to play an insignificant role. That is why you must prepare for and appreciate the effect each person may have on the jury.

Know the Role Each Character Will Play

The active members of your cast are those who will actually say something to the jury. Proper preparation allows you to know what is going to be said. You confer with your witnesses, and you study the discovery of witnesses your opponent will use. If the trial was to be based entirely upon words, you could well predict the effect of all witnesses prior to *voir dire*.

There is more to a character, however, than the words that come from the mouth of the witness. That is why you study the witness during depositions. That is why you study your own witnesses during interview. Imagine those witnesses as very important characters of your courtroom drama.

Know the Role of Those Who Will Not Testify

The judge is the best example trial lawyers know of a character of the drama who never testifies, yet has a great influence upon the jury. That is why you refer to "His Honor's instructions." The jury accepts the trial judge as knowing all about the law, so you use this character of your drama to show that the law is on your side. The jury's view of your relationship with the judge is extremely important.

Make Even "Bit Players" Part of Your Drama

The bailiff who cares for them during trial becomes the jurors' friend, so acknowledge that, and certainly don't appear cold or above this friend of theirs. Other courtroom personnel and even prospective jurors who are chosen, or not chosen, are a part of the drama. Identify with the good guys, and cause the bad guys to be identified with the opposition.

The woman you are impolite to on the elevator may become the forewoman of your jury. The man you are going to strike anyway *can* hurt you if you are disrespectful and a fellow member of the jury panel is offended. The court reporter you snap at is the only person in the courtroom who appears to be working, and jurors sympathize with her.

Recognize the potential importance of every character of your drama. Treat every human being with respect. Try to get those who are hurting you off stage, but those who can help you must be kept stage center.

Play Down the Effect of Characters Who Can Hurt Your Case

You know from the start that certain characters of the drama are going to hurt your case. How much they hurt you may depend upon how much you are able to minimize that witness' role in the drama. A special agent for the FBI is not all that special if every agent for the FBI is a special agent. The doctor on the stand isn't entirely infallible if he can't cure the common cold.

EXAMPLE: MINIMIZING THE ROLE OF AN ANTAGONISTIC WITNESS

We had reached that part of the *voir dire* where I asked the question about the presumption of innocence. A little old man stood up in the jury box and spoke with a foreign accent.

"This is the United States of America, and in the United States of America a man is innocent until he is proven guilty."

The man sat down and the courtroom was dead silent. What more was there to say? A man who came from a foreign country had just given us a brief, but dramatic lecture on citizenship. It made us all wonder if we would not all be better citizens if we went through the process of being naturalized.

Those words permeated that courtroom from the moment they were spoken until the moment the jury retired to deliberate. Even if the man who had been given a "bit part" in our courtroom drama had been struck from the jury, his words would have lingered on and been remembered by those who were chosen to serve. He did serve, however, and a glance at him was a reminder of what he had said.

While the jury was deliberating, I turned to my opponent, who had prosecuted state and federal cases for many years, and said, "Tell me, Noel, how come you didn't strike my little man from the jury?"

"I don't know, Ed. Maybe I didn't have the heart to strike him just because he is a good American citizen."

That might have been it, or what about the effect this would have on the other jurors? Would they not wonder why the state would strike this little old man? Would that mean they have a weak case, or were afraid to let a man who believes in the American Constitution stay on the jury?

ALTERNATE STRATEGY: Strike him! This was one case I wanted to win, because I felt it would be unjust to send this young man to prison. We trial lawyers want to believe we had something to do with our victories, and blame our defeats on other factors, but I must tell you with all candor, this victory went to our constitution, and to the little man who was center stage for less than a minute, but who deserved an Oscar for his performance. The jury returned a verdict of not guilty, and the man played an important role.

We remember many great actors for minor roles they played on stage or in the movies. They give an Academy Award to supporting actor and actress. In our courtroom drama, give a person one line, and he may steal the entire show.

BRING CHARACTERS INTO THE COURTROOM
BY VIDEO

For centuries, the testimony of those who could not appear in court was lost to the trial lawyer. With the advent of discovery, that evidence was not lost, but was presented in an undramatic manner.

During this age of electronics, you can actually bring your witness into the courtroom by video.

Preserve Pretrial Evidence with Video Depositions

Every time you take a deposition, ask yourself if there will be any advantage in making this a video deposition. Cost and other factors may cause you to decide against it, but you should *at least* think about it.

A witness who is elderly and ill, but whose testimony is necessary for a trial, is of course a prime candidate for a video deposition. This should be taken immediately.

Video depositions can also encourage fair settlements. In one case an elderly man, visiting Florida from Canada, drove across two lanes and into the car in which the plaintiffs were riding. By the time counsel was retained, the gentleman had returned to Canada but was reached by telephone. He was nearly ninety years old, and could barely speak.

Negotiations failed and suit was filed. The insurance company refused to pay more than $40,000 and the plaintiff could not even consider such an offer. Arrangements were made for counsel to go to Canada to take a video deposition of this elderly man and to let him speak into the camera and explain why he was travelling across two lanes of traffic and into the side of the plaintiff's car. Counsel knew the jury would look at that video depo and wonder what in the world this old man was doing behind the steering wheel of an automobile. The insurance company must have placed some importance on this same question, because the settlement offer went from $40,000 to $125,000, and the case was settled. Maybe the video deposition that was about to be taken had nothing to do with the increase in the offer, but you will never convince the plaintiffs of that.

Video statements are becoming a very important part of estate planning. I once said I would never have my will drafted by an attorney who did not know how to try a lawsuit, and that requirement is more significant today. Every will is a potential lawsuit, and every video statement is an insurance policy against losing a will contest.

Preserve Evidence of Intent for Future Use

Video statements from clients have become an important part of estate planning. Consider the following:

"Mrs. Jones, I have just drafted your will and I would like to take a video statement, as a part of our estate planning process. Do you have any objection if I do that?"

"No. Of course not."

"You understand that you are now being photographed and your voice is being recorded, and you have no objection to this?"

"That is right."

"And you have no objection to my recording what may otherwise be confidential information, and even using this tape, if necessary, at some future date."

"That is fine."

"I have just drafted your will for you and that will makes no provision for your one daughter living in Philadelphia, is that right?"

"Yes."

"And that daughter's name is Mary?"

"Yes."

"Would you like to explain why you made no provision for your daughter, Mary?"

"Yes, I would. Mary has never visited me, does not write me, even when she lived here, she did not visit me when I was in the hospital—in fact, the only contact I have had with her during the past few years was when she cheated me out of $20,000."

"How did that occur?"

"I put that amount in a joint account for each of my two daughters, with the understanding I would have the money as long as I needed it, but once I was gone, it would belong to the daughters. Well, Mary withdrew that money without my knowing about it and left town."

"Did you give that money to her?"

"Absolutely not."

"Did you intend for her to have the right to withdraw the money?"

"Of course not. It was my money in my account, and she just took it. She stole it. I need that money and she won't give it back to me."

The tape of that video statement will live long after this woman is gone. It will someday come into the courtroom, or to a deposition room, and the daughter will come "face-to-face" with her deceased mother. In nearly all states, the state of mind of a person *is* admissable.

CONCLUSION

Before the use of radar in speeding cases, motorists prayed for something that determined their speed accurately. Motorists have since decided radar clocks their speed too accurately and they aren't really all that excited about knowing how fast they were going. Drunken driving defendants will not enjoy watching themselves on television, and witnesses who lie at a deposition will not enjoy seeing that lie on television. The camera does not lie, it does preserve statements and testimony, and it can be dramatic!

USING VIDEO TO ENHANCE ANY COURTROOM DRAMA

1. Use video to bring unavailable witnesses into the courtroom.
2. Use video to highlight admissions and mistakes of opposing witnesses.
3. Use video to show "day in the life," mechanical functions, and other parts of your story.
4. Recreate scenes through video.
5. Transfer home movies and other means of communication into video for easier showing.
6. Use video to prepare for trial by practicing and preparing scenes you are about to present in court.

CHAPTER FOUR

Structure Your Drama —or Lose Your Audience

CURVE THE PLOT OF YOUR DRAMA

When people talk in a monotone, they put other people to sleep. The trial lawyer who tries his lawsuit without "curving his plot," or building interest, will lose the jury and lose his case.

Structure Your Courtroom Drama

The early Greek playwrights got themselves so involved with so many subplots that toward the end of the play a God machine, which was merely a box, was lowered onto the stage and a Greek god would get out and walk around the stage, making things right, so the play could end.

Over the centuries, playwrights have learned to avoid this problem, yet today in courtrooms throughout America, toward the end of a trial, you will see a trial lawyer sitting at the counsel table, staring at the ceiling, waiting for the God machine to be lowered into the courtroom. Why? Because the trial lawyer has not properly structured his courtroom drama.

This chapter will discuss ways to structure your courtroom drama. *Remember:*

1. Plan the sequence of events.
2. What jurors hear first makes a lasting impression.
3. What jurors hear last is fresh in their minds when they deliberate.
4. The attention span of jurors is limited so the dramatist must constantly change the pace.
5. Your best evidence will have a dramatic impact only once, so choose wisely the exact moment of that "realization."

6. Attention is maintained when the story "moves" from one event to another.

   Example: When a witness takes the stand don't let the "audience" feel he or she is going to repeat what the previous witness said. Start with, "Officer Jones told us what happened right before the man appeared; now I would like to direct your attention to what occurred immediately after that."

7. Clarity is next to godliness, so don't tell a part of your story until you have prepared the jurors with sufficient background.

8. Structure means "form," so make sure your drama is presented in a form that is acceptable and understandable.

   Example: Jurors watch television shows that follow a strict form, so jurors are waiting for certain things to happen. Make them happen, but first let them know what form you will follow. The television viewer today is able to handle two or three plots at the same time, if you don't confuse him or her. Tell the jurors the purpose of everything you do so they can better understand how it is all going to tie together.

A straight line is the shortest distance between the beginning of a story and boredom. You must structure your drama, but you must do it in an interesting manner. Life is full of ups and downs, and jurors, who identify so well with life, follow closely a story that curves.

Map Out the Suspense of Your Drama

It was a hot summer night in a slum area of a big city. A young man ran an errand to the drugstore for his mother. (The jury can already feel the suffocation and sweat of that night.) When the young man reached the drugstore, a few friends suggested a ride in the country to cool off. The jury understands that a cool ride would be a welcome relief.

Make the jury see that he got into the car for a ride to cool off not to rob an old man. It is important that the jury sympathize with your client and realize he was just sitting in the back seat while those in the front seat stopped the car and robbed the old man. The fact that he was in the car is the only reason why he is in court, charged with having committed a crime.

By beginning your story before the robbery, even before the young man gets into the back seat of the car, you have prepared the jury for what happened. They already understand why the young man got into the car, and they can understand that his reason was to cool off out in the country, and not to engage in criminal activity. Once you get your story started, keep it moving.

You must map out a plan as to where your story is going. Then you must decide how you are going to get there. REMEMBER, don't get there in a straight line. Put a little suspense in your drama. Unravel your story with finesse.

Remember, also, that each segment of your courtroom drama is a story within a story. The next time you sit down after the *voir dire*, ask yurself, "Have I just won my lawsuit?" Ask the same question again at the end of your opening statement, and again at the end of your case-in-chief. These are three times to tell your story before you reach final argument.

The use of structuring during *voir dire* may be the most ignored opportunity in trial advocacy. We are so busy doing other things that we often lose an opportunity to tell our story, with full dramatic impact during this segment of the trial. Structuring can bring drama to every part of the storytelling process.

Get There with Drama—How to Hold Your Audience

Structuring means planning, organizing, building, and using each element of your story at the proper place, at the proper time, and through the proper character of your drama. To the client who asks, "Why didn't you let me tell the jury I am a deacon in my church?" you reply, "Because I want your minister to tell the jury that." To the client who asks, "Why didn't you prove that guy lied at the scene of the accident?" you reply, "I am going to let *him* do that on cross-examination."

Put drama into your story by:

1. Using *suspense*, which means letting the audience know there is something about to come, and by not telling all of the story at once.

Example: "Mr. Jones, was there some reason you did not open the door immediately?" After an affirmative answer, follow-up with, "First, tell me exactly where you were at the time this happened." The jurors know you are going to come back to the reason and they are now interested in hearing the answer that you have purposely delayed.

2. Using *finesse*, the way Alfred Hitchcock would to hold your attention. This great director never hit you over the head with anything, yet you admired his "craftsmanship." REMEMBER: An important jury study found the two factors that most impressed jurors with one attorney over the other was whether he was "likeable" and "skillful." Don't hesitate to let jurors know you are a skillful storyteller. They will respect you and love you for it. Jurors simply do not want to be bored.

3. Using DRAMATIC IMPACT. Every part of your drama that has a "dramatic impact potential" must be studied to give it the greatest impact possible. These are the saviors that keep a story from sagging. While giving the details of an accident the witness may say, "At that moment I turned and looked at my little girl, and saw blood coming from her head." Don't save it for damages! It is a dramatic part of your story.

EXAMPLE: STRUCTURING THE DRAMA TO YOUR ADVANTAGE

In a contested divorce case, a client could hardly pay a modest fee, much less pay for the depositions that are so important in every contested matter. Opposing counsel represented the wife and during her direct testimony she told her story well.

This began as a happy marriage and there were the usual financial crises that they met together. Then the husband began drinking excessively and that led to evenings at taverns, which led to evenings with various women. Her testimony ended with the final picture of herself as the faithful wife sitting home nights, caring for the children, and waiting for the wayward husband to return.

It was a well-orchestrated story that followed a beautiful curve, and counsel felt it was time for that curve to break in the other direction. He began his cross-examination by asking,

"Mrs. Jones, you have made some rather serious statements regarding your husband—are you telling the court that during the marriage your conduct was above reproach?"

"Yes."

"You have had no affair or even any contact with another man during the marriage?"

"No. Of course not."

Counsel walked back to the counsel table and picked up a letter, had it marked as an exhibit, showed it to opposing counsel, then approached the witness stand.

"Mrs. Jones, I show you what has been marked plaintiff's exhibit 1, do you recognize it?"

"Yes."

"Is it a letter?"

"Yes."

"Is it in your handwriting?"

"Yes."

"Mrs. Jones, will you read the letter to the court?"

She read the letter and it was, indeed, a love letter she had written to a man during her present marriage. Her story that had risen beautifully to the plateau had stumbled, and headed down, with all the elements of good drama. Nothing could save her now! However, a lack of discovery and a lack of experience in cross-examination caused counsel to ask that one question too many. It is a fact that the worst question that can be asked on cross-examination is one that demands an explanation.

Counsel soon heard the answer that had her story taking another curve, and shooting toward the heavens again.

"I suspected my husband, but I tried not to believe it. After they had come home late one night a few months ago, I found lipstick on his collar the following morning. I was upset and cried, but I wanted to save our marriage, if only for the children. I made up that letter, thinking it would make him jealous and save our marriage. I left it where I knew he would find it, but I thought he would bring it to me, not to a lawyer to use to make it look like I had done something wrong."

There was a lot of drama packed into about half an hour of testimony. That is the kind of stuff of which good courtroom drama is made. However, when structuring drama, stucture it to your client's advantage.

CONCLUSION

Drama is the movement of the story from one perception to another. Keeping that drama rich with design gives the drama the impact that reaches the audience. Planning and execution of the drama increases the probability of that movement being in favor of your client's cause.

GENERAL GUIDELINES FOR KEEPING THE DRAMA RICH

1. Cut from your presentation of evidence all that really isn't necessary.
2. Present the evidence in a sequence that enriches the story.
3. Present each important piece of evidence that is important as though you consider it important, and that is how the jury will perceive it.

WIN THE AUDIENCE EARLY

Playwrights have known for centuries that they have to "grab" the audience early or lose it. Trial lawyers have now learned this verity of life, and of all the recent developments in trial advocacy, none is more important than the need to win the lawsuit as soon as possible.

Include the Need to Win Early
Among the Purposes of *Voir Dire*

The well-cited "Chicago Study" of jury verdicts has prompted trial lawyers to give the first part of the lawsuit the attention it deserves. According to this study, at the conclusion of opening statements, 80 percent of the jurors have reached a conclusion on the question of liability and will not alter that conclusion. When a lawyer now sits down after delivering his opening statement, he is within his rights to break out in a cold sweat and wonder whether or not he has lost his lawsuit.

I remember an English professor saying, "Don't tell me what you are going to say. Say it! Don't tell me this is a fascinating story. Make it fascinating." Trial lawyers are finally learning the wisdom of what the old professor said.

I have seen good trial lawyers spend several minutes explaining to the jury what the opening statement is all about. I see a definite trend, however, toward going right into the story. Good drama requires no explanation.

Make Sure You Have Won by the End of Your Opening Statement

There was a time when defense counsel would "reserve opening statement" until after plantiff's case. The advent of discovery destroyed the possibility of hiding a theory, the only advantage of that practice. The Chicago study has made the practice a real relic of trial advocacy, and it is hard to imagine circumstances under which a trial lawyer would want to "reserve."

What the Chicago study did for opening statement, it should have done for *voir dire*. Lawyers now tell themselves that they have to give a good opening statement because by the end of opening statement they may have won or lost the lawsuit. Opening statement is only half of what happens by the end of opening statement.

Voir dire is a part of the "winning early" concept. This is bringing about a new kind of *voir dire* and increasing need for lawyers and not judges to conduct the *voir dire*. Trial lawyers should make a deal with the judiciary: Let us conduct the *voir dire* and we will settle more cases early in trial, because we will know sooner who is going to win.

REMEMBER: You must overcome a few centuries of lack of appreciation of opening statement on the part of the trial lawyers and trial judges, and you can do this by:

1. Telling your story. You have an opportunity to put words in the mouth of every witness you will put on the stand. There is no way opposing counsel can keep you from not only asking leading questions, but also giving leading answers.

2. Telling your story dramatically. Appellate courts have not been cursed with the misconception that an opening statement must be boring. I am unable to find one decision that says acceptable words are unacceptable if they are said as though you mean it.

3. Being prepared for objections. Some good trial lawyers wait for that first objection before they start the sentences with "Our evidence will show. . . ." Avoid argumentative opening statements, but don't back off because opposing counsel feels you are doing too good a job. Your objective is to tell the story your evidence will tell, and you are permitted to do that. Use "Our evidence will show. . . ," rather than openings such as "We will prove. . . ." Avoid the conflict suggested by "proving" or having to prove something. Telling the jury you are merely going to show them is more positive and will possibly save you from objection.

4. Being sincere and logical. Being persuasive does not depend upon shouting or even being dramatic in the outward sense. Make your words dramatic. You can say "The child lay there in the street in a pool of blood" as softly as you can utter the words, without losing the impact of a single syllable. In fact, shouting those words may sound offensive to the jury. Many objections from opposing counsel are aimed at ineffective overdramatization, whereas a more calm, logical, and effective approach would not have given opposing counsel an opportunity to object.

Once You Win a Case, Keep It Won

Cases are never really won until the jury returns its verdict. When things are going right, keep them going right. That drive toward victory must be handled with care, which means confidence, humility, respect, caution, and all the other qualities of a winner.

EXAMPLE: GETTING A CASE STARTED STRONG

It took two years for counsel to get two busy trial lawyers into the same courtroom, but something is to be learned trying cases against lawyers such as Frank Cleary, then Dean of the Insurance Company

Lawyers, and John Shepherd, 1984-85 President of the American Bar Association. It was a losing case, but counsel gained respect as a lawyer who will do battle for his client.

The next time counsel had a case with Frank, he thought he had a good crack at it, but the insurance company would not offer a dime. He prepared for that trial, and when the case was called, rose and said, "Ready, your Honor," and he was.

The voir dire went well, and the opening statement went well. Then the young lady who was injured in the accident took the witness stand. She had some problems speaking in front of the people, but counsel had worked with her and hoped this could even be turned to her advantage.

She did beautifully, and as counsel concluded the direct, he was proud of her performance. The time had come, however, for her to be cross-examined by the old master. Counsel was surprised as Frank rose and asked for a brief recess before beginning his cross.

His request was granted and he leaned across the table and said, in a half-whisper, "Tell me, what has the company offered you in this case?" Counsel told him, "Not a dime," and Frank said he would make a phone call.

When he came back, the case was setted for $18,000, which was a good settlement in those days, and Frank was not known to be generous with his client's money.

Lawyers like to think that they won their case early, but they are never quite sure. When an offer goes from zero to $18,000 that quickly, counsel knows he was off to a good start. That good start can bring about a settlement, or lead to the big verdict.

It is important that you:

1. Picture the beginning of your drama. The voir dire, opening statement, and that first witness get you into the case. Somewhere during the beginning the ending may occur. Recognize this part of the drama as being the time when you must sell your story.

2. Plan this part of the drama well in advance. Keep a large supply of light cardboard in your office. It only costs a little more than paper, so get a ream of it and keep it handy. When you think of something you want to ask on voir dire or say in

opening statement, type it, punch holes in it, and place it in your trial notebook under "*voir dire*" or "opening statement." Do that for every part of your trial notebook, because the more dedicated you are in preparing that first part of your drama, the better chance you have of not having to finish the rest of the trial.

3. Bring drama into your drama early. Every trial lawyer loves a good cross-examination, or a good final argument. Don't save all your drama for the end. It may be too late! Jurors live in a world in which they can turn a knob and listen to another network, or turn it off and go to sleep.

CONCLUSION

Getting off to a good start is important in anything you do, but it is becoming increasingly important in trial work. Remember, not only can a good start win for you, but a poor start can lose for you.

HOW TO GUARANTEE A GOOD START
IN YOUR COURTOOM DRAMA

1. Don't waste the first few minutes of *voir dire*, use it to help the jury relax and get comfortable, but also use it to start winning your lawsuit.
2. Tell a friend about your lawsuit before trial, and then tell the jury about your lawsuit, in much the same manner during opening statement.
3. Start your case-in-chief with an important piece of evidence.
4. Do all of the above with drama.

REACH THE PLATEAU OF THE DRAMA

Reaching the pleateau of the drama is what the drama is all about. It is that moment of realization when the jury knows what the trial lawyer wants them to know. It cannot come too soon, or too late, if it is to have its full impact.

Build to the Plateau

Once that special plateau moment occurs, you must move on with the story, but the drama is never again quite the same.

As a trial lawyer, you must build toward this, sometimes saving precious evidence until the exact moment when it will have its most dramatic impact. This requires patience, and it requires planning. At the very outset, you must recognize what will cause such a moment, and then decide how to use it and when to use it.

You must realize that his drama does not begin during *voir dire*. It begins the first time your client walks through the door of your office. This means you will be aware of this plateau before the trial begins.

When the trial lawyer hands the insurance company a settlement brochure, or when he shows them a "Day in the Life" film, he may have reached the plateau. That may be the moment in which the drama heads to an immediate settlement, and a good settlement is certainly as good as a good victory in the courtroom.

Recognize the Plateau When You Reach It

When you are taking a deposition, you often reach that plateau of the settlement process. You can tell that opposing counsel is going to call the home office as soon as he can and ask that they review the file again, with the new evidence obtained at the deposition. If you are interested in a settlement, do something while that precious moment is alive. Don't wait for it to lose its dramatic impact.

It is extremely important that you:

1. *Recognize the moment has arrived* by looking for it, by training yourself to find it (watch for that moment in movies, plays, and television programs), and by asking yourself what you would do if you were writing this drama and wanted a moment of realization when the important question would become very clear. Maybe it would be a witness being confused, an entry in a journal that just doesn't seem right, the way a witness is evasive, or the fact a story is simply too perfect. Good trial lawyers look for that plateau, and they find it.

2. *Seize the moment when you have found it.* Don't let an advantage see-saw back and forth, or get away from you. Pin down the witness, dramatize the demonstrative evidence, show the insurance company the jewel that forces them to settle, hold an exhibit high in front of the jury so they can see it. Above all, let your audience enjoy that moment with you, for if you don't it is all for naught.

If the case is not settled and you begin your trial, it is a new drama that is about to unfold, so you must work anew toward the plateau at which you are going to unveil the "realization" the jury must get to if you are to win. What comes before or after, what time of day it is, whether you have properly prepared the jury for it, and many other factors will affect exactly how impressed the jury will be.

Give the Plateau Its Full Dramatic Impact

Plan your plateau, and announce it. Don't take a chance on a single juror missing what is about to happen. The tone of your voice will help notify the jury, and if all else fails, you can tell them, in whatever words you choose, LISTEN TO THIS, THIS IS EXTREMELY IMPORTANT!

Examples: "Doctor, please tell the jury what chances this young lady will have, in your opinion, of ever pursuing her career as a dancer." "Mr. Smith will you please come over here in front of the jury." Give him time to become the center of their attention. "Now, Mr. Smith, will you please remove your shirt and show the jury where the bullet entered your body." "Your Honor, may I pass this photo among the jurors at this time, so they have a better understanding of the scene as I introduce evidence as to what happened at this place." "Mrs. Jones, I know how difficult this is for you, would you like a recess for a few moments?" "No, thank you, I will continue."

MOVING TO A WINNING PLATEAU

EXAMPLE: *A client walked into counsel's office one morning and said he was so concerned about what was happening to his marriage that there was no longer a reason to live. He said he was suddenly* receiving love letters from an unknown woman, and that his wife would not believe him when he told her he was faithful.

When he went to Chicago on a business trip, there would soon be a letter arriving at his home from this woman. She knew much of his personal affairs and he knew nothing of her, or even who she might be.

Counsel asked him if he had ever jilted a woman, and he said the last woman he had anything to do with, other than his wife, was a woman he was dating at the time he met his wife, nearly forty years earlier.

"Was she unhappy about your breaking off with her?"

"Yes, but that was forty years ago."

"Do you have her handwriting on anything? Does she live in this area where her signature may appear on a deed at the courthouse?"

He was not sure, but agreed to find out what he could. The next day he brought counsel a snapshot of him, the woman, and another couple in swimming suits. They had been swimming at the river and had the snapshot made, and they had all signed their names on the snapshot.

Counsel gave his client a big smile and said, "Let me have our handwriting expert look at this."

Within a few days, the client dropped by and was told the good news. At first, he was pleased, but then said, "What difference does it make? My wife will just say, "so your lawyer has hired some expert to get you off the hook." Then he stopped as he was leaving, and turned back and said, "You will NEVER convince my wife."

Counsel smiled and said, "You want to bet?"

Stop! Before reading further, ask yourself what you would do. How can you use this piece of evidence most effectively? How can you convince your client's wife that her husband is faithful? This is what counsel did:

> "I am going to file suit against this woman for $100,000, and I am going to include your wife as a party plaintiff."
>
> "I don't want the woman's money, I want my marriage."

"You aren't going to get any money, you are going to prove to your wife that this whole thing is a fraud, perpetrated by this woman."

"How in the hell am I going to do that?"

"You just wait and see."

About a month later, counsel and others sat around the conference room table. The court reporter was to counsel's left, his client to his right, and his client's wife sat next to him, since counsel made her a party plaintiff. Across the conference table sat this woman, and her attorney.

"Mrs. Smith, I show you what has been marked plaintiff's exhibit 1, which is a love letter. Do you recognize this letter?"

"No."

"Is that not your handwriting?"

"No. Absolutely not."

"Let me show you what has been marked plaintiff's exhibit 2, a photograph. I would like for you to look at this photograph very closely. Take your time and make sure you read the signatures on the photograph."

She was very surprised and became very nervous. She pulled herself together and was now ready to proceed with the questioning.

"Now, Mrs. Smith, I am going to ask you whether or not this is your signature next to this photograph of the person on the left; but first, I think it only fair to tell you that our handwriting expert is prepared to testify that the signature on that photograph and the writing on this letter are from one and the same person."

The witness looked at the photograph and then looked at the letter, and then burst into tears and started shouting, "I am sorry! I am sorry!" Her attorney led her from the room.

Counsel turned to his client who sat there speechless, as his wife started crying and said, "I'm sorry, dear, I should have believed you; I'm sorry."

I just love happy endings like that. It happened that way because things sort of fell in place, but not entirely by accident. When the handwriting expert handed Counsel that little jewel, Counsel had to figure out how to reach that plateau in a way that would give it the dramatic impact it deserved.

You don't have to be a great trial lawyer to do this. You do, however, have to learn how to use your evidence effectively. If you do less than that for your client, you are guilty of malpractice, legally and morally.

Let us consider some ways you can accomplish this:

1. Appraise the value of the evidence. Not what you think it is worth, but what the jurors will probably think. Nothing sinks faster than a moment which impresses the attorney, but not the jury. You simply have to figure out how impressed the jury will be before you decide how much of a fuss to make over it. This comes with experience, but a good substitute for experience is simply showing an exhibit to friends, or asking what they think of a certain part of testimony.

2. Once you know its value, give it whatever prominence it deserves. WARNING, what your client thinks should be "played up" is often the last thing you want to use with such drama. Good trial lawyers have a way of stopping the trial and directing attention to what is about to come. Learn that technique. THINK what you are about to do is important, and the jury is likely to get the idea.

3. Let the evidence be great, and your saying it is great is no substitute. You can highlight the moment, whether it be testimony or an exhibit, but the real moment of greatness must be the evidence itself. If the jury is disappointed in what you are highlighting, you either did not choose something that should have been highlighted, or you did not present it properly.

CONCLUSION

The end of your drama will be preceded by a plateau that you must recognize and appreciate. From that moment on, you are "wrapping it up." When you reach that plateau you should have won your case, so build toward it and save the victory, once you have acquired it.

HOW TO RECOGNIZE THE PLATEAU IN YOUR DRAMA

1. You will have proven all you are required to prove;
2. You will have filled in your story with the human factors that will cause jurors to want to decide in your favor;
3. Look for that moment when you know that prolonging the telling of your story will involve more risk than benefit; and
4. Watch the jury and make sure you stop before interest wanes.

MAINTAIN THE JURY'S INTEREST

The trial of a lawsuit is not the most exciting thing that has ever happened to the people sitting in the jury box. The newness of jury experience soon wears off and it is difficult to hold the jury's interest. Jury trials are seldom as exciting in the courtroom as they are in movies and on television.

Use Drama to Get the Jury's Interest as Soon as Possible

Never take the jury's attention for granted! Neither you nor your lawsuit will automatically obtain the jury's attention. Use drama to get the jury's attention and use drama to keep it.

Nothing you do in the courtroom should be done without considering its effect upon the jury. If you object as though you don't care, jurors may wonder why you are objecting. If you ask questions on direct or cross as though you aren't interested in the answers, they may wonder why you asked the questions. The best way to maintain the jury's interest is to let them know you *are* interested, that you think this is important.

There is no way you can keep the jury alert during every minute of the trial. Signal the jury as to when they can relax, as to when they must listen closely, and as to when it is extremely important that they listen.

Examples: "Your Honor, I have these fifteen documents that I need to introduce as exhibits, I have had them marked, and it will take a few minutes for Mr. Smith to identify them for the record." If the jury doesn't take a few minutes off after hearing that, they may never have another chance during the rest of the trial. "Officer, will you describe for the jury the condition of this woman's body when you arrived at the scene?" Pay attention! During final argument counsel says, "One statement made during this week-long trial tells you all you need to know in this case." The least the jury can do is listen for one moment if they are about to hear all they need to hear.

Plan Your Trial to Intersperse the Most Interesting Parts of Your Evidence

Interesting evidence should not be bunched up at the same time. Long periods of nothingness can lose a jury forever. Plan also not to give important evidence to jurors when they are least receptive, such as when they are anxious to go to lunch.

From the theater, we can adopt many ways of keeping the audience's attention. The range of the voice of the person talking is a simple way. Monotones are monotonous, but that is only the beginning of voice manipulation. Raising your voice can attract attention, but lowering your voice can be even more dramatic. Sudden silence also can be effective.

The use of physical evidence gets attention. Varying the mode of presentation, such as use of video instead of live presentation, is useful. Remember, anything you do will not keep the jury's attention for long, so you must be constantly changing your act.

Keep an Eye on Jurors to Determine When the Drama Most Needs a Shot in the Arm

When you can tell the jurors are bored, it may be too late—you may have lost them. Keep an eye toward the jury to determine if they are becoming bored. If you see you are losing them, do something different, because you must be doing something wrong.

Five simple ways to accomplish this are:

1. Change from oral to demonstrative evidence. "Officer, you have described what happened, did you obtain any physical evidence at the scene?" Immediately, the jury listens. Was there a gun? What is in that box sitting on the counsel table? Is there some proof that does not depend upon one person's word against another?

2. Change the scenery. Get up from the counsel table and walk to the end of the jury box. If you are tied to a podium, take a piece of evidence up to the witness so the scene moves from the podium to the witness stand. Have the witness come from the witness stand to the blackboard. Activity tells the jury your drama is moving, and they must at least turn their heads to keep up with the action.

3. Go to a more interesting character. The jurors have heard expert testimony all morning, and they have grown a bit tired of it. "Your Honor, before I call the next engineer, I would like to call John Smith who was actually at the scene when my client was injured." This suggests a change, and it suggests an "eye witness" account, a courtroom term that has so impressed people that many television stations have adopted it.

4. Go to a more interesting part of the testimony. Much of a witness's testimony is routine dialogue that is necessary to help you "get to the jury," yet a part of that testimony is also dramatic. How fast a car was going, the exact location of one car compared with another, whether a driver put his foot on the brake immediately, and the exact direction a car swerved are all tedious elements of tort liability. They simply do not compare with such testimony as, ". . . I was then thrown against the window and I heard my little child shriek with pain." Don't lose your audience before reaching the people part of your story. Be flexible! Insert a few questions that will keep the jury alert to the fact this is a human situation involving human beings, and not abstract principles of law that belong on a law exam.

5. *Stop the trial.* That is exactly what I mean! "Your Honor, I think if we took a five-minute recess I would save considerable time." Always save time for the Court—it's your best reason for halting the proceedings. Every trial judge will swap you five minutes for half an hour. However, impress upon the judge that you have marked exhibits and have done everything else in advance to avoid delays, but this one could not be avoided. If you have to approach the sidebar to settle a certain matter, do it while the jury is not attentive. Get rid of such delays in the trial when you want to stop the trial. Don't wait for the big dramatic moment and have it interrupted with a sidebar conference while the jury sits waiting.

EXAMPLE: KEEPING THE JURY ALERT

Criminal lawyers are imaginative because they become very desperate as they sit at the counsel table, knowing their client is heading for prison as they sit there doing nothing. They feel an urgent need to do something.

A number of years ago, at a St. Louis County Bar Christmas party, I was talking with Judge Amandus Brackman and Charlie Shaw, the criminal lawyer. The judge asked, "Ed, did I ever tell you what Charlie did to me during a criminal trial? When I finished my instructions, Charlie told the jury, 'That is not the law in Missouri and don't pay a bit of attention to what the judge says.'"

"What did you do, Judge?"

"I was so astonished that this young lawyer would do such a thing, I forgot to hold him in contempt of court."

Charlie told me that on another occasion he sat at the counsel table listening to the prosecutor give a final argument that seemed certain to send his client to the gas chamber. He couldn't just sit there and do nothing, so he jumped up, grabbed the prosecutor by the arm, swung him around, and shouted, "That's a damn lie, and you know it." The scuffling was soon subdued, but the mood was broken.

Those who specialize in criminal law are sometimes unorthodox, but you must admit, they are dramatic!

Warning: *Such tactics include a great amount of risk, and attorneys must find other ways to meet such a crisis. In addition, never try to imitate another attorney's style, adopt your own.*

Suggestions:

1. *Protect your record* so an appeal can be made if the judge erred.
2. *Make your objections,* to protect your record, in the event opposing counsel abuses the process.
3. *Represent your client vigorously* so the jury knows you are not play-acting without entering that precarious area that may subject you to contempt.
4. *Anticipate disastrous situations* to see if they can be avoided, including plea bargaining, to avoid the agony felt by counsel and client at the end of a criminal trial.

CONCLUSION

Keeping the jury alert throughout the trial is a challenge, but one that deserves your attention. You should be in control of your drama, and if you are we will orchestrate it at a pace that will keep it alive and emphasize what will help your cause.

DRAMATIC HINTS FOR KEEPING THE JURY ON THEIR TOES

1. Remember, jurors want to perform their duties well, and look to you for guidance.
2. Constantly give the jurors priorities as to which witnesses are important, which issues are important, and which evidence is important.
3. Change the pace to retain interest.
4. Intermingle demonstrative evidence.
5. Move the activity to various parts of the courtroom.
6. Do it with drama.

DON'T END THE DRAMA BEFORE THE FINAL SCENE

With all the recent emphasis on winning early, you must be careful not to lose sight of your objective—the final scene. Beginning lawyers want to win when they explode an opponent's case during cross-examination; and some television viewers still expect the real murderer to rise in the audience before the first witness is sworn. The truth is, the final argument is where the courtroom drama should end.

Build Toward the Final Scene of Your Drama

Saving the best for last is the best way to maintain interest. You must not only do this, you must let the jury know you are doing this. Hint, throughout the trial, that there is more to come.

Use cross-examination as a groundwork for final argument. You are not permitted to explain anything during cross-examination, and you certainly don't want the witness to be explaining anything. Be patient and save that explanation for the end of your drama.

You don't build toward something, once you have passed it. Know what your goal is and work toward it. Know when you want to reach that goal and try to arrive on time. Study every play or movie you see, and appreciate the way the writer has kept you interested by building the drama and saving something for you to look forward to.

Save Something for that Final Dramatic Moment

Ending your drama too soon is like stopping a beautiful song in the middle of it, or stopping a drama just as you are getting interested. No playwright would treat his audience that way, and no trial lawyer should treat the jury that way.

Build! Build! Build!

Outline the building of the drama:

1. During *voir dire*, acquaint the jury with the drama.
2. During opening statement, tell the story.

3. During your case in chief, build the drama.
   (a) Your client was a nice looking young lady who was beginning a bright career.
   (b) The other party was intoxicated and drove into the side of your client's car.
   (c) Your client was seriously injured, but tried to resume her career.
   (d) Witnesses tell the story of how this valiant attempt was in vain, that she is no longer able to function.
4. On cross-examination, *discredit their story.*
   (a) Defendant tries to explain his conduct but must admit that he had been drinking and did not even see the car in which your client was riding.
   (b) Defendant's doctor testifies he could find no permanency, but admits he only examined her a short time and admits such a loss of use of the arm could result from such an injury.
5. *Conclude dramatically with the final argument.*
   (a) Cover the logical steps that prove your case.
   (b) Fill in with that which has the most dramatic impact.
   (c) End with the "Final Five," that is the most dramatic and convincing reason you can give in five minutes as to why you should win and win big!

   WARNING: Don't waste final argument reviewing testimony witness-by-witness, and don't waste final argument on what you didn't prove, or anything else that won't dramatically end your story.

Maintain Interest by Letting the Jury Know that There Is More to Come

Lawyers enjoy giving final argument, and jurors usually consider this the best part of the trial. Don't rob the jury of this treat by bringing it all together too soon. Let them know that you are going to end with a final argument that will end this dispute, once and forever. Then use your final argument to accomplish just that!

EXAMPLES:

1. *During opening statement tell your story, but also tell the jury this is just the beginning. "The doctor will tell you exactly what he found when he examined the child."*

2. *During direct examination, use your witnesses to let the jury know what is coming now and what is coming later.*

> "Officer, did you discover anything else when you arrived at the apartment?"
> "Yes. A blood sampling."
> "Is that what you turned over to Dr. Smith?"
> "Yes."
> "Dr. Smith will tell us about that; did you find anything else?"

3. *Use cross-examination to set the stage for final argument and for further evidence.*

> "Mr. Jones, you have denied that you know a man named David Williams?"
> "Yes, I do."
> "Are you sure you will not recognize David Williams if he appears here in court today as a witness?"

EXAMPLE: SAVING DRAMATIC IMPACT
FOR THE LAST MOMENT

It was two days before Christmas as I stood in the courtroom of Judge William M. Corrigan. Standing along side me was a young man who had committed several burglaries and who was about to learn his fate, at this, the sentencing. The prosecutor refused to recommend probation and the presentence investigation report recommended against it. It was not my speech to the court, but the judge's response and sentencing that was dramatic.

Not one person in the entire courtroom could tell whether or not the young man would be placed on probation until the final moment of the sentencing. After reviewing the young man's conduct and history, the judge said, "If I were to put you on probation, I would do you no favor. If you serve your five years, you will owe the court nothing. But, if I place you on probation, you will walk out of this courtroom with a key in your pocket.

"That key is to the state penetentiary in Jefferson City. You will carry that with you wherever you go. If you violate any provision of your probation, that key will open the door to the state penetentiary, and that is where you will live, not for five years, but for fifty years."

Notice the symbolism used by the judge. It was beautiful. I could picture that key, and it was very large, so large that the young man would always be cognizant of its presence, so large that others would notice it.

The judge's use of the key was effective. His saving the decision till last was especially effective. Remember, if the judge had told us early in his remarks that he was going to grant probation, he would have lost his "audience." It was a beautifully orchestrated sentencing, and one that held every person in the courtroom until the very last word.

CONCLUSION

Remember, every segment of your trial is a "play within a play." Your *voir dire* should not end too soon. Your opening statement should not end too soon. Your case-in-chief should not end too soon. Your final argument should not end too soon. Build up to what you want to be the plateau of your drama, then get as much dramatic impact from it as you can. Then sit down!

HOW TO ACQUAINT, UNFOLD, AND BUILD YOUR DRAMA TO JUST THE RIGHT POINT

1. Let the jury know what you are going to show.
2. Use *voir dire*, opening statement, and your case-in-chief to start building your drama.
3. Once you have reached the magic moment when you have accomplished what you set out to do in that segment of your drama, stop!

TELL PART OF YOUR STORY WITH WITNESSES

During the *voir dire*, the opening statement, cross-examination, the physical evidence of your case-in-chief, and during final argument, you are unveiling your drama by telling your story. All of this is extremely important, but none of it detracts from the fact most of your story must be told through the oral testimony of witnesses YOU put on the stand.

Recognize the Importance of the Oral Testimony

Don't become too sophisticated in the art of trial advocacy! Don't be so busy looking for new ways to present your drama that you ignore the very basis of your drama—the dialogue that comes from your cast. No playwright would make this mistake!

Make Testimony the Central Part of Your Drama

When you plan your drama, plan the action around what your witnesses say. You may want to use physical evidence to prove what could have been proven orally, but that physical evidence cannot just appear on the scene—good dialogue must get it there!

Build Other Evidence and Argument
Around Your Oral Testimony

Use *voir dire* and opening statement to build up to oral testimony. Let the jury know what oral testimony will be given, and where it is safe to do so, let them know the character from whom the dialogue will come. If you know the minister is going to testify your client was with him at the time the crime was committed, let the jury know that such evidence is going to be presented so they can look forward to its presentation.

ALTERNATE STRATEGY: Some excellent trial lawyers will "play" with the jury and build suspense, and use that dynamite evidence without forewarning the jury. If you use this approach, stop immediately before the big surprise and get the jury's attention, so they will appreciate the full impact of this dramatic moment.

What is important is—that you use it with drama. This is not just oral testimony, it is the kind of dialogue that can bring real drama to the courtroom. Treat it as such!

There are two steps you must remember:

1. *Prepare the witness to give convincing testimony.*
   Avoid a scene that looks "too prepared" for that sin is nearly as bad as being "unprepared." Prepare without looking prepared. Have a witness tell the story to you several times, and make sure he uses words the witness would normally use. Look for what is believable and ask yourself if that is probably how it happened.

2. *Present the tesimony with drama.*
   As you prepare the witness, look for words the witness uses that are sincere, typical of that witness, and dramatic. Words, phrases, and even incidents you hear as the witness tells you the story should be analyzed and used according to how much dramatic impact each will add.

   EXAMPLES: "When I saw my little boy in that condition, I cried." "He got out of the car and stumbled toward our car." "Yes, I heard what she said, but she was crying so I couldn't understand every word."

3. *End the testimony with drama.*
   A good actor or actress must learn how to get off stage. Keep a good question that will not prompt re-cross to end the testimony to use as the "last word."

   EXAMPLES: "Mrs. Jones, this lawyer has asked you a lot of questions about what you saw; now did you see the truck prior to the collision?" "There is no way I could have seen him the way he came out of that alley."

Let the Jury Know the Importance of Oral Testimony

Most of your drama is going to be oral testimony, so prepare the jury from *voir dire* to expect your proof to come from oral testimony. Older jurors lived by the radio, but younger jurors have been trained on television and must adjust to "exposition." Since you must depend on oral words, use them dramatically, and let the jury know that words are dramatic.

EXAMPLES: "Dr. Smith will tell you about this condition." "You will hear from an eyewitness exactly what happened." "I am going to read from a deposition the very words used by this man when he admitted he was wrong." "Listen to this young man as he tells you what happened." "Six witnesses are going to testify and each one will tell you what happened that night."

Let Your Client Tell His Story—If Possible

The jury want to hear your client *tell his story*, and, with rare exceptions, your client wants to tell his story. Sometimes you can't put him on the stand, for such reasons as a criminal record that will haunt him, and sometimes when you do put him on, you want to get him off as soon as possible, since he may not be helping his cause. However, your client's testimony, or lack of testimony, is a critically important part of our courtroom drama, so don't forget its importance to the jury.

Use Your Supporting Cast—Dramatically

Eye witnesses, favorable experts and even character witnesses form a supporting cast that causes playwrights to dream and imagine. Playwrights love to give such characters the kind of dialogue that would move the jury and bring life to your drama. Don't pass up this splendid opportunity.

EXAMPLE: *GETTING WITNESSES TO SUPPORT YOUR CASE*

I had served as mayor of a city in which the police department boasted of a two-minute response time. An officer of that department was called by opposing counsel to testify relative to his investigation of an auto accident. My cross-examination consisted of one question:

"Officer, this lady who had the accident with my client claims it took your police department ten minutes to arrive at the scene of the accident. Do you believe that?"

"I certainly do not," the officer replied.

Oral testimony of police officers can be extremely important, in civil as well as criminal cases. Get what good you can from them, but get them off the witness stand before they can hurt you.

There are many witnesses who can tell your story:

"Did you see the car driven by Mr. Jones immediately before it came in contact with Mrs. Long's car?"

"Yes."

"What did you see?"

"I saw his car come out onto the highway and run right into the lady's car."

Dialogue of an eye witness can establish liability!

"Do you have an opinion, Doctor, based on a reasonable degree of medical certainty, as to what effect, if any, the injury will have on Mrs. Smith's employment?"

"Yes. It is my opinion that due to this injury Mrs. Smith can never work again at the kind of work she did prior to the injury."

Dialogue from your expert can prove damages!

"Where were you at 8:05 p.m. on the night of May 5?"

"I was attending a class at night school."

"What time did you arrive at school?"

"About seven o'clock."

"What time did you leave?"

"About 9:30."

"Who was your instructor that night?"

"Mr. William Jenkins."

"Is he in the courtroom?"

"Yes. That is him sitting in the front row."

Dialogue from your client can keep him or her out of prison!

CONCLUSION

Tell your story with the dialogue from the witnesses you put on the stand, and build your case around that dialogue. Imagine for a moment that there is no physical evidence, and there are no statements or arguments to be made by counsel. If your oral testimony can stand by itself, then you will have something to talk about in final argument.

**REMEMBER THESE POINTS ABOUT WITNESS DIALOGUE
TO GAIN THE MOST DRAMATIC EFFECT**

1. Make sure the witness talks to the jury.
2. Make sure the witness uses words the jury will understand.
3. Make sure the time and place of words and sentences give full dramatic impact.
4. Give the "good lines" to the witness who will present them with most drama, even if it is an adverse witness who will be making a statement favorable to your cause.

USE PHYSICAL EVIDENCE WITH DRAMA

Playwrights have said for centuries, "Don't tell them, show them!" Demonstrative evidence is relatively new in the courtroom, but its value is being appreciated. It not only adds drama, it varies the pace and adds another dimension to your presentation.

Decide What Part of Your Drama Can Be Presented with Physical Evidence

Good active dialogue is better than exposition, the explaining of what happened. Even good active dialogue, however, needs all the help it can get. Physical evidence is a good source of that help.

Examine every element of your proof to find what can be proven with physical evidence. If you can make your proof *without* physical evidence, still use the physical evidence. The law of evidence calls it real evidence, and that is exactly what it is. Use it!

Don't let the physical evidence come in as an afterthought. Don't let it be cumulative! Lead up to it and let it be the dramatic moment of that scene!

Decide When Physical Evidence Will Have Its Most Dramatic Impact

Decide whether or not you want it to sit on the counsel table before being introduced as evidence. You may want the jury to wonder about it and build up any expectation. You may want it not to detract from what is happening prior to its introduction, and save the first sight of it for that dramatic moment. Most of all, you do not want the jury to get used to it, which would lose its dramatic impact.

Decide whether you want to use it on your direct or while cross-examining an opposing witness. When you walk up to the witness stand during cross-examination and say, "I hand you what has been marked plaintiff's exhibit 10 . . ." the jury expects something damaging to that witness, and is ready to give that exhibit its full worth.

Present Your Evidence with Drama

How you handle an exhibit will affect the amount of dramatic impact it will have on the jury. Don't expect the jury to accept it as something special if you don't treat it as something special. You would hardly have the doctor laughing as he explained an X-ray, or have a woman smiling as she identified a photo of the car in which her husband was killed.

You might want to have an exhibit passed among the jurors while the witness is still on the stand. Sometimes by the time the juror sees the exhibit, it has lost its impact. Tie the exhibit into a certain part of the drama by introducing it and passing it when it will have the most dramatic impact.

EXAMPLE: USING PHYSICAL EVIDENCE FOR IMPACT

A circuit attorney for the City of St. Louis prosecuted a case in which a hat that was found at the scene of the crime sat on the counsel table throughout the trial. Neither attorney asked the defendant to try on the hat. The prosecutor was afraid it would not fit, and defense counsel was afraid it would fit. Yet, its presence there had a powerful impact.

That is something a trial lawyer must remember about physical evidence. The jury places much importance on it, so you had better know in advance whether a hat fits before you ask someone to try it on. If it doesn't fit, the jury may disregard all of the other convincing evidence upon which the state relied.

Even the lack of physical evidence can be a factor. This occurred in a case in which one lawyer depended upon oral evidence to question the integrity of a document, including a deposition from California. He set up the opposing counsel for an easy final argument, which went like this:

> "My opponent has questioned this written document, and he had introduced oral testimony to prove his case. In fact, he brought into this courtroom a deposition taken all the way out in California.
>
> "Have you not wondered during this trial, as I have, why he went all the way to California to take that deposition, when he could have walked right across the street from this courthouse and walked into the office of one of the best handwriting experts in the world. This expert could have told him if there was anything wrong with this document and this lawyer could have put this expert on the witness stand with his exhibits that would prove the document is no good.
>
> "But you didn't see any handwriting expert testify. What if they took this document to a handwriting expert and he found nothing wrong with it. You don't think they would put him on the stand and tell you the document is perfectly good. So, we don't know whether they took this document to a handwriting expert as they normally would; or do we?"

CONCLUSION

Use every weapon in your arsenal. The law of proof will demand of you as much oral testimony as a jury can possibly absorb in one trial. Use your imagination! Use physical evidence, and use it dramatically!

POINTS TO REMEMBER WHEN USING
DEMONSTRATIVE EVIDENCE

1. While preparing for trial, examine every piece of possible demonstrative evidence.
2. Do not use demonstrative evidence that might hurt you.
3. Do use demonstrative evidence that neither hurts nor helps build your story, if it adds drama or interest.
4. Use demonstrative evidence at the moment it will receive most dramatic impact.
5. Keep that evidence before the jury only as long as its dramatic effect is continuing to build. (If the jury no longer notices it, you left it there too long.)

CHAPTER FIVE

Design the Set
for Your Drama

KNOW THE SET FOR YOUR DRAMA

The courtroom is but a stage, and all of the lawyers, witnesses and others will act out their roles on that stage. The trial lawyer should have this stage in mind, as he or she prepares for trial, and proceeds through the drama.

Know Your Stage

Take a look at Figure 5-1 and study the "stage" given to us by those who design courtrooms. This is not exactly like every courtroom, but it is very similar to many courtrooms.

In the courtroom, we shove the audience over to the side of the room. There are only twelve (sometimes six) members of the "audience," and this is why their numbers have delegated them to a less important part of the courtroom.

The judge sits in an elevated position and lawyers know the importance of this. Jurors in some courts, especially in certain foreign countries, also have an equally elevated position, but that is an exception to the rule in the United States.

You will present your drama more effectively if you take advantage of the "theater-in-the-round" atmosphere in the courtroom. This design, copied from certain theaters, permits the trial lawyer to move between the judge, the witness stand, and the jury. This is especially true in jurisdictions that do not restrict the trial lawyer to a podium.

You are the leading character in the courtroom drama, and should use to your advantage the fact you are surrounded on three sides, that is by spectators on one side, the jury on another, and the judge and witness stand on the third. This gives you an opportunity to be surrounded by action.

Figure 5-1   Set Design—The Courtroom

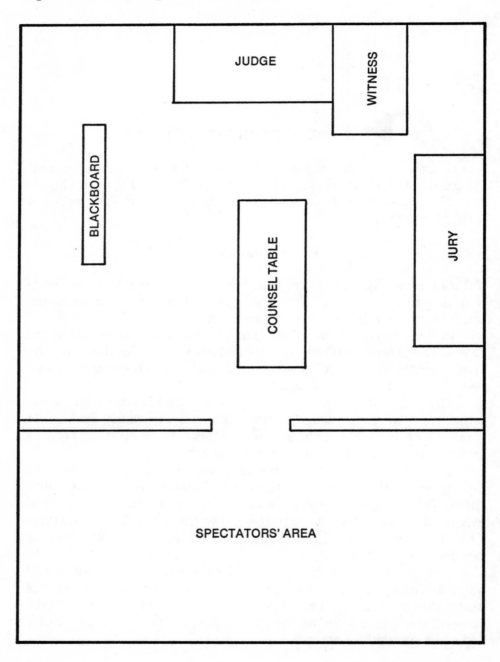

Where you take the action is very important, and this is why you must always keep in mind the "areas" in which you will operate. You can focus attention on the bench by references to the judge or through conferences at the bench. You can take the action to the witness stand, where most of the activity will occur. You can point to the back of the courtroom by asking, "Would you say you were about as far as I am from the back of the courtroom?" The blackboard area can be the location of charts and exhibits. One advantage in using the blackboard as a blackboard is that it creates action. You are doing something, and when you have a witness come from the witness stand to identify something, or write something on the blackboard, there is further action.

Keep in mind that your counsel table is the middle of this theater-in-the-round. Everything that happens at the counsel table is seen by the jury. You may not want your client sitting at the counsel table. You may not want to keep exhibits there for the jury to wonder about while they should be listening to evidence. If your client is at the counsel table, you may not want him or her within proximity to be giving you messages, even though you have warned against this.

In courts in which you have a choice of the counsel table, you should exercise that choice wisely. Sit on the opposite side of the counsel table so you can have eye contact with the jury without being obvious. Observe the jury panel during *voir dire*, and observe the jury during the entire trial. Some lawyers like to sit near the jury, feeling an advantage in that proximity. One flamboyant criminal lawyer did this so he could mumble messages that he felt could be heard by the jury and no other person in the courtroom.

EXAMPLE: STAGING YOUR DRAMA TO WIN

"I was standing about as close to him as I am standing to you people." This abstract sentence from the transcript of a trial tells us more than mere testimony, it tells us something very important about the staging of this testimony.

The witness was talking to the jury. She was not talking to the attorney who had asked the question. She did not say she was about as close to him as to the attorney. It is very important that witnesses talk to the jury, and it is important that you as the trial lawyer encourage this kind of dialogue.

"Mrs. Jones, will you please tell the jury . . ." The witness is encouraged to tell the jury, not the lawyer. Those who design courtrooms may shove the jury to the side, but we must do something about that. We must direct the action, including oral testimony, toward the jury.

The "audience" at the trial is the "trier of the fact." We must always keep our audience in mind, and know exactly where that audience is, and how all else must revolve around it.

CONCLUSION

Know the courtroom in which you are going to try your lawsuit. If it is a new courtroom, get the feel of it before the day of the trial. This is your stage, this is where you are going to perform. You must feel at home in it if you are going to win.

**THE COURTROOM IS CHANGED AT THE LAST MINUTE—
HOW TO IMMEDIATELY FEEL AT HOME**

1. You must always be psychologically prepared for trial by dismissing the "homecourt advantage" myth, and know that your experience has prepared you for any change.
2. When you prepare for a particular stage, you also must consider possible changes that may occur and prepare for them.
3. You must request time to adjust to any change, and be prepared to explain to the judge the need for this time.
4. You must object to any change that can be avoided and would cause harm to your client's cause.

MAKE THE STAGE YOUR OWN

Actors and directors "own" the stage upon which they operate, and they adjust it to serve their dramatic needs. Trial lawyers must adopt the same approach and turn the courtroom into the stage they must dominate.

Once you have well in mind, the stage upon which you are to operate, focus in on where your action will occur and who will become a part of that action. There is no better place to start than to study Figures 5-2 and 5-3 and learn the importance of eye contact during direct examination.

The left side of this figure portrays the direct examination in which the attorney and witness are stage center and all else does not matter. The lawyer asks the question, looks at the witness, then the witness looks at him and answers him. The jury is on the sideline and is not included in this action.

The right side of this figure portrays the proper way to examine a witness. The attorney looks at the witness while asking a question. The witness is looking at the attorney. The attorney then looks at the jury and this causes the witness to look at the jury. Then the jury looks back toward the attorney when he asks the next question and so does the witness.

Direct the Action within the Physical Structure of the Stage

What we have accomplished by turning this dialogue into a triangle that includes the jury in the conversation is the expansion of the stage. We not only include the jury in the conversation, we include them in the area of activity. Eye contact is extremely important, and including the jury in the action is also important. You can accomplish this without moving a stick of furniture or a single person.

Make Physical Changes as Required

Keep your eyes on the jury and see if there is something they need. Is something obstructing a view? Is a woman cold as she sits in the wind of an air-conditioning vent? Can the end juror see an exhibit that is in a far corner of the courtroom? Is the sound portion of the videotape loud enough?

If you need to move something so a juror can hear, see, or be more comfortable, do so. If the jury is losing interest because all activity has taken place at one location for too long, do something about it. You are the stage director—place people and objects in the courtroom where they will have the greatest dramatic impact.

Figure 5-2   Eye Contact—Direct Examination
                        (improper method)

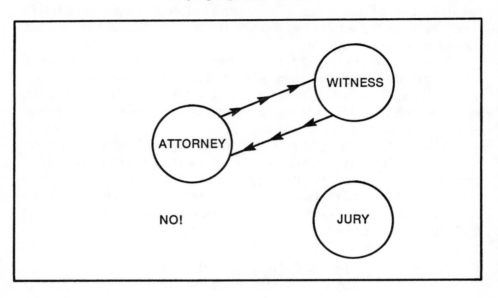

Figure 5-3   Eye Contact—Direct Examination
                        (proper method)

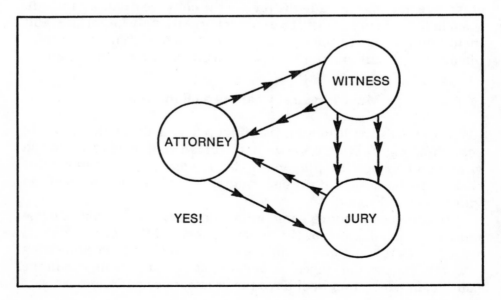

EXAMPLE: *Showing an X-ray through a viewing box will add some drama to the presentation, yet it will limit the jury's view of the X-ray. By passing the positive of the X-ray among the jurors, you have moved an activity from the distant location right into the jury box.*

Respect the Judge's Control of the Courtroom

The judge has complete control over the courtroom, and a trial lawyer should never forget that. Trial judges, however, recognize the need for lawyers to use the courtroom and to make adjustments from time to time. Use discretion! Before moving an object or rearranging the courtroom, request permission if there is the slightest chance the judge may object. Explain the need!

HISTORIC EXAMPLES LEADING TO CHANGES IN THE COURTROOM STAGE

Do you know the answers to these courtroom trivia questions?

Q. In which famous American jury trial, did the judge recess the court to the lawn outside the courthouse?

A. In the 1923 trial known as the "Scopes Monkey Trial." The presence of such people as Clarence Darrow and William Jennings Bryan in the small town of Dayton, Tennessee, and the controversial issue of whether or not evolution should be taught in the schools, attracted large crowds that increased the heat of the courtroom, and tested the strength of the building, causing the judge to reconvene on the courthouse lawn.

Q. During what senate hearings did members of the underworld, and lawyers representing them, come into living rooms of America through television for the first time, making "I refuse to testify" a household response?

A. The Kefauver Committee hearings.

Q. During what senate hearings did the lawyers complain of television cameras situated between them and the witnesses they were interrogating?

A. The McCarthy Committee hearings re communism.

Q. What ever happened to Rule 35?

A. Rule 35, recommended by the American Bar Association, prohibited the use of cameras in the courtroom. All states once followed the rule and most states still do. My own state of Florida was a leader in permitting the use of cameras in the courtroom, and many states have followed. There are serious questions that have been raised as to the effect this will have on the trial of a lawsuit.

Florida has permitted cameras in the courtroom by rule change, *Chandler* v. *Florida*, 449 US 560, 66 LEd2d 740, 101 S. Ct. 802, and other states have reached the same result through the trial judge's discretionary powers. *Brooks* v. *State*, 244 Ga. 574, 261 S.E.2d 379; *People* v. *Spring*, 153 Cal.App. 1199, 200 Cal.Reptr. 849. However, by rule, statute and case decision, most courts do not permit cameras. *Fitzmorris* v. *Lambert*, (La.) 377 So.2d 65; *Mazetti* v. *United States*, 518 F.2d 781.

There is a disadvantage to working under a microscope, but there is also the advantage of those being viewed by millions making sure they perform at their best. Cameras in the courtroom have the distinct advantage of letting citizens watch the judicial process, especially when the entire trial is televised.

Cameras in the courtroom put pressure on the judge, jury, and witnesses, but they also make the trial more dramatic. For centuries, those who work in the courtroom have developed some sloppy habits that they do not want to expose to the world. Televising a few trials will not bring great change, but when televising trials becomes commonplace, trials will become more efficient.

The need for drama in the courtroom will increase as the use of cameras in the courtroom becomes more widespread. Cameras point up the need that stories be told in a more interesting manner. If a camera never reaches your courtroom, the need is still there, so you must recognize that need and so something about it by bringing drama to the courtroom.

Why are these trivia not so trivial? We have seen much change in the courtroom and its activity, and we have seen ways in which courts have adjusted to various circumstances. We can expect the future to bring many more changes that will affect the stage upon which we present our drama, and we must understand these changes and adjust to them.

CONCLUSION

The judge will, by rule or custom, provide the stage upon which your courtroom drama will appear. The judge will also control any changes in the physical arrangement and use of his or her court-room, but all of this is subject to reasonable change upon suggestion of reasonable attorneys. Adjust that courtroom to your needs so it can function effectively as the stage of your drama.

THINGS TO BE AWARE OF AS YOU SET THE COURTROOM STAGE

1. The jury is your audience, and all that happens in the courtroom must be for its benefit.
2. The jury must be able to see and hear all that you want it to perceive.
3. You must bring the action close to the jury to establish intimacy, without invading its territory.
4. Plan the location of your exhibits, blackboard, television, and other parts of your stage so you have the action flow to those parts of the courtroom.
5. Know in advance exactly where you and others will be during each part of the drama.

CHAPTER SIX

Use a Dramatic Prologue

USE SHAKESPEARE'S PROLOGUE CONCEPT
TO WIN MILLION-DOLLAR VERDICTS

Shakespeare introduced his characters with a prologue (intro-duction) and brought a new form of drama to the world that lawyers have now discovered. Prior to 1962, there was no such thing as a million-dollar verdict. As trial lawyers have discovered the prologue, such verdicts have become commonplace.

Use Your Opening Statement to Tell Your Story

Picture yourself sitting in the jury box. You want to know what the lawsuit is all about. Use your opening statement (the lawyer's prologue) to immediately tell your story in an interesting, exciting way, within the boundaries of "law and custom," with drama!

EXAMPLE:

> "On January 1 of this year, Bill went to the home of a fellow student, John Williams. When John went into the back-yard, Billy went with him. What Billy did not know was that the Williams kept a dog in the backyard, and that dog was an Afghan hound.
>
> "Our evidence will show that the dog charged at Billy and Billy tried desperately to climb the fence but the dog reached Billy and the huge and curved teeth of the dog bit into the right arm of Bill and tore flesh and skin from that arm. I will show you photos of the dog's teeth, and photos of the tear in Billy's arm."

Counsel has immediately told the jury what the lawsuit is all about. He has dramatically shown Billy trying to climb the fence, with the jury hoping he will make it. Counsel then tells the jury Billy did not make it and describes the teeth and the tear, and promises to show the jury photos that the jury now anticipates. Once, as he began the second paragraph, he uses a "our evidence will show" to avoid objections that he is "arguing his case," yet the phrase does not hinder the progress of the drama.

Tell Your Story within the Boundaries of Law and Custom

I say within the boundaries of "law and custom" because many trial judges have a "custom" of exceeding the law in preventing trial lawyers from presenting the opening statement with too much drama. The opening statement is not an argument. However, that does not mean it must be sterile, restrained, or boring.

Tell the theme of your story during the first few paragraphs. Don't leave the jury hanging with, "I know this is a nice lady and I am sorry she was injured, but please, Mr. Attorney, tell me why this company should pay her $100,000."

Give the jury the why, and then the how much. Give them the liability, and then the damages.

Structure your opening statement, as you structure your entire courtroom drama. Make it self-sustaining. Imagine, for a moment, this is all the jury is going to hear. Don't say, "I'll cover that later." Tell the whole story during opening statement. The jury may not be convinced with less, and the purpose of opening statement is to convince.

Use opening statement as more than a prologue, not less. You do care who wins. Win, and win early!

Here is an example:

"The doctor has testified at deposition that he left the clamp in Mrs. Johnston's body. He further testified that the leaving of the clamp in a patient's body is certainly the kind of 'treatment' that falls short of proper medical standards in this or any other community." At the very outset, at the beginning of opening statement, counsel resolved any question as to liability and can now direct the jury's attention to the important question of how much his client suffered as a result of this negligence.

Use Opening Statement to Introduce Your Characters

Introduce leading characters you know will testify. Never promise the jury something you may not be able to produce. This may devastate your credibility and credibility is what a lawsuit is all about.

The leading characters you introduce, should include the "bad guy." Tell the jury, "Mr. Smith has admitted at the deposition that he was driving on the wrong side of the road, so there will be no conflict on that question," or "I expect Mr. Smith to testify he was on the right side of the road, but if you listen to his testimony, I want you to remember that he testified under oath at his deposition that he has been convicted of perjury, but, of course, maybe he wasn't telling the truth when he said that."

ALTERNATE STRATEGY: Skip the ". . . but, of course, maybe he wasn't telling the truth when he said that." Some trial lawyers use "cutesy" tails on the end of sentences effectively, while others fall on their face.

Since you are the leading character of your courtroom drama, introduce yourself. Don't say, "I'm Ed Wright." They know that by now, and they weren't all that fascinated the first time they heard it.

Tell them who you are through the delivering of your opening statement, by what you say, and how you say it. What you really want them to know about you is that:

1. They can believe you.
2. You are sincere about your cause.
3. You will show them why they should decide in your favor.

If you can accomplish this, the jury will feel comfortable about the trial, and anxious for it to begin. You will have used your prologue effectively.

**Win Your Case by the End of Opening Statement—
Or You May Never Win It**

The Chicago Study revolutionized the opening statement. The most significant conclusion reached by the study was that 80 percent of the jurors make up their minds on the question of liability after opening statement, and do not change it. When you finish your opening, chances are you have won—or you are finished.

EXAMPLE: MAKING POINTS DURING OPENING STATEMENT

"At twelve o'clock noon, Josephine, sitting here at the counsel table, fixed lunch for her children and her father-in-law. By one o'clock she had cleared the table, sent the children off to school, and sat down to watch her favorite television program.

"She knew she must leave her home by 2:00 P.M. to catch a 2:10 bus a few blocks away. She had a 2:30 appointment at the special school district and was assured the bus would get her there in time. So, a few minutes before two, she turned off the television and walked out the back door and down an alley, and by two minutes after two she would reach the intersection of Pendleton and Brentwood Boulevard.

"At twelve o'clock noon on that same day, January 29, 1979, John Horton was having lunch with a customer at the Sunset 44 Restaurant and Lounge. John Horton is the sales manager of the company the client is suing, and after having lunch, and a few alcoholic drinks, he got into his automobile and left for an appointment in Westport Plaza.

"John Horton drove his company car east from the lounge, and then headed north on Brentwood Boulevard. He would arrive at the intersection of Pendleton and Brentwood Boulevard at exactly two minutes after two."

This parallelism caught the jury's interest. They knew something was going to happen at exactly two minutes after two, and that it was going to happen at the intersection of Pendleton and

Brentwood Boulevard. They were prepared for, and interested in the event that this lawsuit was all about.

Counsel then explained the position of his client as a pedestrian, and related, with reference to the driver's deposition, the course travelled by the driver. He explained what the driver did wrong and what he did not do to have avoided running into the client.

Then, but not until then, the jury was ready to hear what happened to the plaintiff. They wanted to know what happened to her, because they now were concerned about her. The jury was then told how the plaintiff was dragged on the front end of the automobile for a distance of 165 feet. The story created the atmosphere of the ambulance arriving and people looking down at her, as she lay on the pavement. It now was time to explain the medical testimony the jury would hear.

The blackboard was used to explain this testimony. It provided an opportunity to, in effect, say, "We know this woman is entitled to be paid for her injuries, now let's talk about how much."

"Our evidence will tell you about five different stages of this woman's life, from the time she was struck by this car until that time in her life when she would no longer expect to work.

"First, (writing on the blackboard) let's call this stage 'intensive care.'" The words three weeks away were written along that line.

"Then, on line two, the second stage is 'Additional Hospital,' which is a period of 13 weeks, from the time she left intensive care until the time she left the hospital.

"Next, on line three, 'Cast from Waist Down' ('three months'). This covers from the time she came home from the hospital until the time the cast was removed.

"Then, on line four, 'Additional Period of Pain, 13 months.'

"Finally, on the bottom line, 'Unable to Work' and next to that '32 years.'" This covers the time until she is 65 years old. Evidence will show that her earning capacity has been affected, and that she will never be able to perform the duties she performed prior to her injuries."

This outlined the medical testimony, and throughout the trial, with evidence and argument, these spaces would be filled in with dollar signs. This trial occured in Missouri, a state that does not permit per diem argument, but does permit a "period of time" argument. Assigning dollar amounts to certain periods of time can be very effective, having many of the advantages of the per diem argument, without the legal objections found in most jurisdictions.

SUGGESTION: Don't say "cast," say "cast from waist down." Be descriptive, even if it takes a few more words on the blackboard. Give each period of time the drama it deserves. Don't just say "hospital" if part of the time was spent in intensive care. Give your client credit for all of the time spent in intensive care, or any similar experience. Remember, intensive care often means a period of "touch and go," and it often means a period in which the injured person and the husband or wife cannot communicate. This can be a frightening period of time, and one that should be conveyed to the jury during opening statement.

EXAMPLE: MAINTAINING MOMENTUM
WITH DRAMA

After completing the opening statement, the attorney began the case-in-chief. The witness was telling the jury the same story that had just been told to them, but without the drama.

The jury was losing interest, so the attorney walked back to the counsel table and picked up a photograph and handed it to opposing counsel. The jury was following this action. The photo was shown to the witness.

"Mrs. Jones, I have handed you what has been marked plaintiff's exhibit 1. Do you recognize it?"

"Yes."

"What is it?"

"It is a photo of the intersection of Pendleton and Brentwood Boulevard."

"Does this photo fairly and accurately represent that intersection as it appeared at the time you were struck by this man's automobile?"

"Yes. It does."

"Would you take this pen and make an X *on the photo where you were standing at the time of the impact?"*

"Sure." *The witness marks the photo.*

"Now, will you mark your name alongside that X, *so we can remember what the X stands for?"*

"Sure." *She marks the photo.*

The attention of the jury has now been recaptured. They are ready to hear the oral testimony. For another "shot in the arm," stop and ask that the photo be accepted into evidence. When it is done, turn to the judge and say, "Your Honor, I would like to pass this exhibit among the jurors at this time so they can visualize the scene better and follow the testimony of this witness."

There is no reason the judge should refuse such a request, although some may to save time. If you are at a low-attention point, it would be difficult for a juror to fall asleep while looking at a photo. Once again, well into the testimony of the first witness, the momentum had been strong, but again a juror became a little bored.

The attorney walked back to the counsel table and reached into a brown paper bag and took out some clothes that had dried blood all over them. The attorney approached the witness stand and showed them to the witness after having them marked and showed them to opposing counsel.

"I now show you what has been marked plaintiff's exhibit 2. Do you recognize this exhibit?"

"Yes. It is the pair of jeans I was wearing when the man hit me with his car."

"What is the red stuff on the jeans?"

"Blood."

The jury had listened carefully during the opening statement. That is what you want from an opening statement. However, your drama cannot sag when you sit down after the opening statement. Your opening statement is a promise that something is about to happen.

CONCLUSION

Introduce your drama to your audience! Let them know what is to come—let them expect! Let them want to learn more! Tell them through your *voir dire* and then through your opening statement that this is going to be something important, and something they will want to hear about.

HINTS TO ALWAYS KEEP THE DRAMA UPMOST IN THE MINDS OF YOUR AUDIENCE

1. Remember the short attention span of jurors.
2. Remember most of what you are presenting is foreign to their daily experience.
3. They do not know how the trial is going to proceed, and will appreciate your keeping them informed as to what is going to happen when.
4. Signal priorities to the jurors so they can alert themselves to what you want them to consider as very important.
5. Eliminate from your drama all that is neither dramatic nor necessary.

FOLLOW UP AFTER THE OPENING STATEMENT

If you have won by the end of the opening statement, you want to keep it won. If you have not won, you have your work cut out for you.

Plan What Is to Come
Immediately After Opening Statement

The first witness to testify attracts attention because the jury knows the trial is beginning. That interest vanishes within minutes, if the testimony is not interesting. Give constant thought as to how you will maintain interest.

You may want to save a good witness for a little later when the drama needs a shot in the arm, but don't start with your worst witness. START WITH A GOOD WITNESS! The jury may decide after hearing one witness exactly how much attention it will give the other witnesses, and it may decide exactly how good your case is going to be.

Remember the importance of primacy. What a witness hears first is what will have the most lasting effect. Every attorney wants to get in the first jab, and in the courtroom a trial lawyer should never give up that opportunity.

Remember the three objectives of your testimony, to create atmosphere, develop character, and advance the plot. All three must be done early in your trial. Once you explain in opening statement what you are going to prove, advance immediately toward that proof.

Characterize your evidence before trial. An exhibit that proves exactly what the oral testimony will prove may be a "shot in the arm" that can be used when oral testimony seems to be putting the jury to sleep. A piece of paper signed by the witness may be "devastating" evidence that is going to blow him right out of the chair. Two hours of records that must be introduced in order to "make" your case may be "tedious testimony" that must be injected with as little pain as possible.

A doctor's background may be "impressive" and worthy of your giving it full dramatic impact. One of your witnesses may be "disgusting" and you want to get his evidence to the jury with as little damage to your cause as possible. Certain testimony may be "surprise" evidence and not introduced until the right moment. A defendant's admission may be "conclusive" evidence that you will use as soon as you are ready to "wrap up" that part of your case.

Include Some "Good" Evidence Early in the Drama

Once you understand the character of a piece of evidence you can decide at what stage of the drama you should use it. If you are to win early you may be wise to use good evidence early. Timing is important, structuring is important, and winning early is important! Don't save too much for later!

Keep the Momentum of Your Drama Going

Momentum is important! Don't lose it! You can relax after the trial. Build up to the next plateau of your drama. Don't let it sag!

CONCLUSION

Shakespeare loved the prologue, but he also loved to follow up with drama that mankind had never before perceived. Let your *voir dire* and opening statement tell your audience that your courtroom drama is about to really take off! Then follow through!

GUIDELINES FOR MORE EFFECTIVE PRESENTATION
OF *VOIR DIRE* AND OPENING STATEMENT

1. Begin *telling* your story at the beginning of *voir dire*.
2. Begin *explaining* your story during opening statement.
3. Start introducing the characters of your drama during *voir dire*.
4. Start building credibility for you, your client, and your cause, during *voir dire* and opening statement.
5. To let the jury become bored during any part of the trial is unwise, to let them become bored during *voir dire* or opening statement is unforgivable.

CHAPTER SEVEN

The Courtroom
Is Your Stage—
Dominate It

USE THE "BLOCKING REHEARSAL" CONCEPT

The director of a play often begins with a "blocking rehearsal" at which he reviews the script, telling each member of the cast where he or she should be on stage during each part of the dialogue and action. This important technique from the theater can be applied to your courtroom drama with amazing results.

Plan Your Blocking in Advance

A trial lawyer often proceeds with his drama with no concern as to where the action is taking place and whether the jury is directing its attention toward the desired place.

If there is any distraction in the courtroom, do not proceed until you eliminate it. If two spectators in the front row are laughing during a serious part of the trial, give the bailiff time to get them out of the courtroom before you ask the next question. Then ask an unimportant question to recreate the mood before continuing.

You can avoid mistakes often made by trial lawyers if you plan your blocking in advance. If necessary, draw a diagram of the courtoom and place your "cast" on your "stage." Study Figures 5-1, 5-2, and 5-3 of Chapter 5, and have in mind at all times a picture of the courtroom and how it relates to the stage of a theater.

Use Blocking to Direct the Jury's Attention

One excellent way to direct the jury's attention to a person is to have that person look at the jury. In Figure 5-2, during direct examination, the attorney and witness look at each other, and the jury is not a part of the conversation.

In Figure 5-3, the attorney looks at the witness, asks a question, and then looks at the jury, which causes the jury to look at him or her. This triangle of eye contact is extremely important, and its effectiveness can be further assured by occasionally saying, "Now, Mr. Jones, tell the jury what you saw when you opened the door." This will remind the witness to look at the jury, and not at you, the floor, or the ceiling.

Remember—You Are the Central Figure of Your Drama

If rules or customs tie you to a podium, you must still find ways to add action to your role, because you are the central figure. Go back to counsel table for an exhibit. Hand an exhibit to a witness, and stay there waiting for your exhibit, so the jury can have a "group picture" of the witness and you.

Be Prepared to Adjust Blocking to Meet Challenges During Trial

Regardless of how well you plan your blocking, you must be ready to adjust during trial. That is why courtroom drama is even more fascinating than drama in the theater. The script changes, and you never know what might happen next.

For example, you had planned on reading the questions from a deposition and having an associate read the answer from the witness stand. At the last minute, the associate is not available.

If you read the questions and answer from the counsel table or podium, the testimony will not be "coming from the witness stand." Sit in the witness stand, look at the jury, and create the atmosphere of live testimony.

EXAMPLE: SETTING THE STAGE AND ARRANGING EFFECTIVE BLOCKING

Let's apply to the courtroom what we have been discussing. Here is an example from a criminal case.

The attorney rose from the counsel table and walked slowly to the far end of the jury box, as far from the "browbeating" area as possible, and spoke softly.

"Mary, did you come to court this morning with your mother?"

"Yes."

"While riding over in the car did you, and your mother talk about this case?"

"Yes."

"Did she tell you what to say?"

"Yes."

The attorney had hoped for these three answers of "yes." During the voir dire, the attorney hinted that the reason this ten-year-old girl had accused the client of assaulting her was that the girl's mother hated the client because he had refused her attentions. Now the attorney had permitted the ten-year-old witness to explain to the jury that she was merely telling them what her mother had told her to say.

It did not take long for the jury to find the client innocent, partly because of this cross-examination. But what was so unusual about the cross-examination? The attorney asked questions that could easily be answered with a "yes," but stopped when he got the answer he wanted and saved the rest for final argument. He never gave the witness an opportunity to explain, hedge, or change her mind.

The scene was properly staged. The blocking was exactly as planned.

All trial lawyers like to walk up to the witness stand and hand the witness an exhibit, look down at the witness, tower over him or her, and dominate the scene. There is nothing wrong with this at the right time, but this was a ten-year-old girl being cross-examined. Every ounce of sympathy is heading toward that witness and against the attorney who is about to cross-examine her, so he or she must plan the staging.

Here is the staging that worked in this case:

1. *Counsel rose slowly.*
2. *He walked to the far end of the jury box.*
3. *He spoke softly to the witness.*
4. *He talked to her as though talking to his daughter.*

ALTERNATE STRATEGY: *Some jurors expect more than this subtle approach—especially from a flamboyant attorney. It would not be the style of some attorneys to pass up the chance to drive home dramatically the fact that this witness was a parrot for her mother. If you do take out after such a witness, make sure it is the mother and not the girl who is the villain of this scene.*

If injuries are catastrophic and the client sits there for several days, the jury may get used to seeing the client's injuries and the shock will wear off. There is much more of an impact where the jury anticipates the seriousness of the injury and sees the resulting evidence only for a short time, at the moment of testimony and again during final argument. If it is difficult for a person to sit for more than a short time, and she or he has so testified, it doesn't do her or him any good to have her or him sit at the counsel table day after day, showing the jury that she or he can do it. She or he will suffer physically during the trial, and financially at the time of verdict.

Even if the client is seated at the counsel table, the attorney must be constantly conscious of the fact that the jury is looking at her or him. Melvin Belli tells of a witness who had a terribly scarred bald head and sat in the courtroom throughout the trial wearing a wig. Mel made several references to the scars on her head, and painted an awful picture for the jury to imagine, but did not show the jury the bald head with scars during the entire trial.

When the trial ended, he could sense that the jury wanted to see what was under the wig, and he could sense that his own client could not figure out why he had not asked her to remove it. Opposing counsel was certainly not going to ask her to do so. Then, after the final argument, and in typical Belli fashion, Mel turned to the judge and said, "Oh, I'm sorry, Judge, I forgot to show the jury the woman's head." Then he turned to his client and had her remove her wig, and the jury saw for the first time, and only for a moment, the awful condition caused by the defendant.

Decide How the Words Will Be Spoken

Minor stage directions appear with the dialogue, such as (softly), (forcefully), or (loudly). This tells you how you should be speaking at a particular moment.

Decide Where on Your Stage
Various Actions Will Occur

If you use an X-ray the action relative to that x-ray will occur at the X-ray box. If you use a positive of the same X-ray, you can move the action right into the jury box. Counsel can move around the courtroom, or have witnesses move around the courtroom, and thereby move the place of the action, building to a moment with all the patience required of any master of any art. Mel helped the woman put her wig back on, and it didn't quite fit, and she sat there with a slightly tilted wig hiding conditions she would have to live with for the rest of her life. Tears came to her eyes, and the jury noticed.

CONCLUSION

The attorney, and every other member of the "cast," must be placed in the right spot at each moment of the drama. They should move from one part of the stage to another, as will most effectively advance the client's cause. Every word that is spoken, and every action that is taken, will affect the outcome of the courtroom drama. What happens in that courtroom, and where it happens may make the difference of victory or defeat.

GENERAL RULES FOR STAGING THE DRAMA TO WIN

1. Plan your staging in advance.
2. Alter your staging as your drama progresses.
3. Discuss staging with your client and witnesses before they take the witness stand.
4. As you move about the courtroom, keep staging in mind.

ORGANIZE YOUR STAGE DIRECTIONS
AND EXECUTE THEM

The playwright includes in his script, stage directions that tell the cast what, where, and how they are to carry out the dramatic action and dialogue. The "characters" of your courtroom drama, including yourself, need the same kind of direction.

Figure 7-1   Script of Courtroom Dialogue and Action

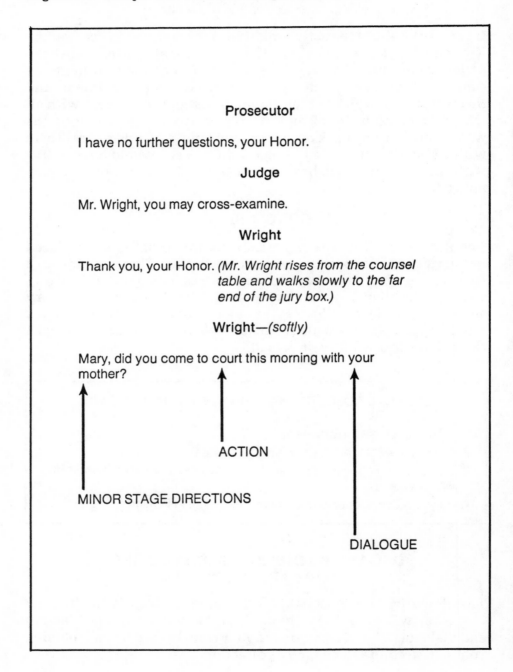

Organize Your Stage Directions
by Picturing Them in Your Mind

The best way to organize your staging is to picture the drama as a playwright would. He could have taken the cross-examination scene of the ten-year-old and written out a script something like the one in Figure 7-1.

One advantage to thinking about stage directions is that often a stage direction will bounce from the page and cause you to question whether or not this is what you want to be doing. If it says (screaming), you might well ask yourself what you are doing screaming at the jury. If it says (sarcastically), you might begin adding up the number of cases lawyers have lost through the use of that one stage direction.

Decide Which Action Can Accompany Dialogue

By looking to the right side of your script, you not only see what action is to take place, but you see very graphically an absence of action. Sometimes you realize you have completed several pages of nothing but dialogue and the jury is finding it hard to concentrate.

Look to the right side of your script, and put some action there! Immediately you must imagine:

(The attorney walks to the blackboard, pauses, looks at the witness and continues his examination.)

Lawyer
Dr., will you tell the jury the name of this dreadful disease you have been discussing?

Doctor *(looking to jury)*
Yes. The name is Impecunimania. (The lawyer writes the word on the blackboard and the jury looks at the blackboard in horror. The attorney returns to the counsel table or podium and continues his examination.)

By keeping one eye on your script, you have been prompted to take two steps that will keep the jury's attention:

1. You have complemented your dialogue with action.
2. You have shifted the action to another part of your stage, which is good drama, in that it adds another dimension and causes your "audience" to *focus in* again.

EXAMPLE: SHIFTING THE ACTION
TO RECAPTURE INTEREST

The attorney rose from the counsel table and walked to the side of the courtroom and picked up a chair. He placed the chair right in front of the jury box, yet far enough back from the jury box that every juror could see. He then continued his cross-examination.

"Officer, would you please come over and sit in this chair?"

"Sure," and the officer came from the witness stand to the chair and sat in it.

"Would you please imagine that this chair is the front seat of an automobile, and sit in it, as though you were sitting in the right side of the front seat of an automobile?"

"Yes."

Counsel walked over and put one end of a tape measure at the officer's right foot.

"Now, officer, will you please take the other end of this tape measure and place it at your heart?"

"Sure," and the officer placed the other end of the tape measure at his heart.

"Now, officer, will you tell the jury how many inches it is from your foot to your heart when you are seated in this position?"

"It is 37 inches."

"Now, officer, you testified earlier that you shot at the rear tire, is that right?"

"Yes."

"And you testified that the distance from the back tire to my client's foot would be about seven feet, is that right?"

"Yes."

"And it is only 37 inches from the foot to the heart when seated in that position?"

"Yes."

"Then you came much closer to shooting this man in the heart than in the tire you were aiming at, is that right?"

"Yes, I guess so."

The trial judge has complete control over the physical arrangement of the courtroom. However, he or she will permit you to make reasonable changes that will help you explain your case to the jury. Before making substantial changes, ask the judge in advance.

ALTERNATE STRATEGY: *You might accomplish the same effect by taking a video deposition of the officer and showing it to the jury. Advantage: You will know in advance how cooperative your witness will be. Disadvantage: You will lose some of the drama of a live performance.*

CONCLUSION

Dialogue is important, but it is only a part of the drama. How you say it, where you are when you say it, and what you are doing when you say it are equally important. THE ONLY WAY you can be sure that you have properly prepared yourself for trial is to make sure you have planned your staging and blocking thoroughly. You need not do this in writing, but once you can picture how it would look if it were written out, you can move through the drama as though the playwright and director were right there, helping you through each dramatic moment of the trial.

NOTES TO HELP YOU ALTER
YOUR STAGING AND BLOCKING

1. Move action to another part of the courtroom to keep attention.
2. Direct action to the bench if that is where a favorable event will be more effective (if only pointing to the bench while saying the judge has instructed (or will instruct you) that . . .).
3. If custom or practice ties you to a podium, move closer to the jury by leaning forward, by changing your level of voice, and by finding excuses to get from behind the podium.
4. Remove a client or witness from the courtroom when their presence may detract from your staging.
5. Move exhibits in and out of "stage center" as they will add to or avoid subtracting from your drama.

Figure 7-2   The Trial Lawyer's Dress Code

1. Choose one of the following as a non-solid color:

   _____ suit   _____ shirt   _____ tie

   SORRY, you can only choose ONE!

2. Choose one of the following colors for your suit:

   _____ dark blue   _____ gray   _____ Other*

   *Choose sparingly and with great discretion.

3. A well-dressed trial lawyer tries to dress _____ notch above others.

   The answer is ONE, not two, three, or four.

4. Female trial lawyers should:

   (a) Dress to project the image they want;

   (b) Dress in what is comfortable for them in which to work;

   (c) Follow local rules and custom, OR CHANGE THEM.

5. Which of the following should be considered, when choosing a suit to wear in the morning:

   ( ) Appearing before judge, or jury,

   ( ) Appearing in urban, suburban or rural area,

   ( ) Racial mixture or the jury panel,

   ( ) Economic status of most jurors,

   ( ) Age group of prospective jurors.

   ALL OF THE ABOVE!

COMMUNICATE—VERBALLY AND NONVERBALLY

Throughout the trial, you are communicating with the jury, verbally and nonverbally. There are specific steps you must take to make sure the communication advances your client's cause most effectively.

Never Forget That You and "Your" Cast Are Communicating Every Moment

The trial of a lawsuit is communicating to the jury your client's cause. This includes communicating a single piece of evidence, and it means communicating to the jury constantly a hundred other things that you want the jury to know and believe.

When a lawyer walks into a courtroom, he starts communicating even before he says a single word. The way he or she is dressed, the way he or she walks, the expression on his or her face tells the jury something about the lawyer who is about to begin the task of establishing credibility and making the jury believe his or her case.

Jurors Will Form Opinions Based On Your Personal Appearance

Recent studies have found that juries are most affected by (1) whether they like an attorney, and (2) whether the attorney is skillful. "Liking" someone they have never met may depend on the personal appearance of the attorney.

How an attorney "appears" to the jury may depend on:

1. The clothes he wears (jurors feel lawyers should dress "appropriately"); see Figure 7-2
2. Whether he seems "comfortable" in the courtroom
3. Whether he is considerate of everyone in the courtroom
4. Whether he is concerned for his client (if he isn't, why should the jury)
5. Whether he is friendly, and a smile is an excellent sign of friendliness

6. Whether he is sincere (credibility depends upon sincerity, and success in the courtroom depends upon credibility)
7. Whether he is humble (juries do not like to return verdicts for lawyers who think they are better than the jurors)
8. The way an attorney moves around the courtroom (he must appear to be confident, comfortable, and skillful)
9. The expression on his face (he must set a mood)
10. What he is doing when attention is focused elsewhere (some juror is looking at the attorney, and is forming an opinion as to whether the attorney is play acting or is genuine)

Ask friends who have served on a jury to tell you about the lawyers who tried the case. You will find out what impressed the juror and what did not.

Communicate Confidence to the Jury

Confidence is one characteristic that you want to communicate to the jury. When you walk into the courtroom, look as though you belong there, you know what you are doing, and you are going to win!

You Must Show Concern for the Jury

A jury will decide in your favor if they like you, so your first job is to get them to like you. One way to do this is to try to help the jury—let them know that you are concerned about them. If a prospective juror obviously doesn't want to be on the jury, try to get him or her excused. Frankly, you don't want people on the jury who don't want to serve. If a prospective juror has any kind of problem, you want every person in that courtroom to know that you are concerned.

Smile in front of a jury—it's important. Smiling is important when you are in the midst of a serious matter. The attorney, his witnesses, his client, and everyone should be very serious.

You and Your Cast Must Project Your Message

Every witness you put on the witness stand is playing an extremely important role. For a witness to speak so she or he cannot be heard, or to talk so fast that she or he cannot be understood, simply does not get the job done. Timing is extremely important in the courtroom.

EXAMPLE: PLANNING THE DRAMA TO KEEP THE JURY ON YOUR SIDE

There are many ways to communicate the wealth of the defendant to the jury. Start by considering why the jury should hear the evidence. First, is it admissible from the standpoint of relevancy, and then is it advantageous from the standpoint of trial tactics?

If the evidence is clearly admissible and the defendant is guilty of conduct entitling the plaintiff to punitive damages because of intent and malice (in the legal sense), it is to your advantage to communicate wealth. The size of the verdict could be based on the defendant's wealth, since it would take a larger verdict to teach a lesson to a wealthy person than it would to a poor person.

From the voir dire through the opening statement and through the plaintiff's evidence, build up to the introduction of evidence relating to wealth. Talk about and then prove what was done was wrong, and show that the defendant knew it was wrong. Then hint that a part of all of this was caused by the wealth of the defendant. Then you will face the problem of communicating the wealth of defendant to the jury.

PROBLEM: No one likes to ask another how much he or she is worth. For a someone to sit on the witness stand and be asked about his or her personal finances is rather "tacky" and lacks the usual class expected of a good trial lawyer. Even a very wealthy person may receive some sympathy from a jury if he or she is forced to answer such questions.

Wait until the very end of the plaintiff's case, and the staging could go something like this:

Judge
Is that the plaintiff's case?

Attorney
I have no further testimony, your Honor (pauses as though what he is about to say is an afterthought), but I would like to read to the jury questions and answers two and three of the defendant's answer to interrogatories.

Judge

You may do so at this time.

(The attorney walks to the counsel table, picks up the answer to interrogatories, and walks slowly to the front of the jury box and reads.)

Attorney

Question 2. How much did you receive last year from dividends alone?

Answer: $128,000.

Question 3. What is your present net worth?

Answer: Four million dollars.

The attorney had waited until the jury knew they were going to find the defendant liable and that they were going to assess punitive damages. They had some hint that wealth was a factor, and were curious to find out exactly how much.

There was no one sitting in the witness stand. If a juror wanted to glance at the counsel table and look at the defendant, he or she could, and a few did, but there was no pressure on anyone. Relieving that pressure from everyone in the courtroom and letting that piece of paper and the plaintiff's lawyer be center stage was the way the attorney had planned it, and the best way to communicate this bit of evidence to the jury.

ALTERNATE STRATEGY: There are other ways to accomplish this, including calling the defendant as your witness. Remember, however, before you reach the ultimate question, to prepare the jurors. They should be ready to assess punitive damages and should want to hear the evidence they are about to hear.

CONCLUSION

From the moment you walk into the courtroom until the jury retires to deliberate, you must communicate. Do this in the way you look and the way you act, and the way the other "characters" of your drama look and act. What you and your witnesses say and how you and they say it will determine how much you have communicated.

GENERAL COMMUNICATION GUIDELINES
TO PUT YOU ON THE WINNING SIDE

1. You must look like a lawyer and act like a lawyer if you expect the jury to perceive you as a lawyer.
2. You must tell your story in a way the jury will understand it.
3. You must present your drama as though every word and every act is aimed at creating an impression favorable to your client and his or her cause.
4. You must appeal to common sense and to human emotions—that is, the best in a human being.

CHAPTER EIGHT

Use Dialogue to Tell Your Story

TIME DISCIPLINE MUST GOVERN
YOUR COURTROOM DRAMA—
MAKE EVERY WORD AND ACTION COUNT

Time discipline can help you keep your audience during your courtroom drama. The judge will limit the time you have for each segment of your drama, but more importantly the juror's attention span will limit the time in which you can present certain evidence or deliver a particular argument.

Know the Purpose of Each Word

A trial lawyer often can play to an empty room, even in a crowded courtroom. Courtroom drama *is* drama. Drama means action, not exposition.

I once sat in a courtroom and noticed that the judge, the clerk, and one juror appeared to be sound asleep. I listened to the words that were putting the entire courtroom to sleep. The dialogue went something like this:

> "Doctor, will you tell us how many times my client visited your office?"
> "Let me check my file."
> The doctor spent five minutes thumbing through notes, and finally answered.
> "Did each of those visits relate to this accident?"
> "No."
> "How many related to this accident?"
> "Let me check my file."

The doctor spent another five minutes checking his file. If you think an expert witness is too busy to discuss the case with you before trial, imagine how he or she hates to waste time and be embarrassed while on the witness stand, and each word of an expert costs you money.

EXAMPLE: THE IMPORTANCE OF A WITNESS'S WORDS

"Officer, did you see the defendant on the day in question?"
"Yes."
"What time of the day or night was it?"
"It was 10:07 P.M."
"And where was he?"
"He was proceeding west on Main Street."
"Was he driving an automobile?"
"Yes, a 1980 Chevrolet."
"Did you notice anything unusual about the manner in which he was driving?"
"Yes."
"What did you notice?"
"He was travelling at a high rate of speed."
"Were you able to determine the speed at which he was travelling?"
"Yes."
"How did you determine that?"
"I followed him for three blocks, travelling the same distance behind him, and my speedometer read 50 mph during the entire time."
"What is the speed limit on that section of Main Street?"
"30 mph."

You have just convicted a motorist of speeding, probably under the laws of about every state of the Union. City prosecutors are able to present their evidence in a few words, because it would be impossible to operate a municipal court without such speed and efficiency. If this horrifies the public, let us look at the evidence required to convict a young man of murder:

"Did you watch the defendant as he proceeded toward John?"

"Yes."

"Did he talk with John?"

"Yes."

"Did you hear what they said?"

"They argued over a girl for a minute or two."

"Then, what did you see?"

"I saw Jim reach into his jacket and pull something out."

"Could you see what it was?"

"Yes."

"What was it?"

"A knife."

"What did the defendant do next?"

"He stabbed John in the chest with the knife. Twice."

"What was John doing, right before he was stabbed?"

"Nothing, just talking."

"Anything else?"

"No."

This plus a little expert testimony sent a young man to prison for murder. It doesn't take many words, it just takes the right words presented in the right manner.

Prove your case with as few words as possible, so you will have time to add words that will bring drama into the courtroom. You may want a witness to remain center stage longer than required for the proof he or she is offering, because he or she is adding drama. Give that witness the extra time and deduct time from the process of methodically presenting evidence that must be presented to prove the case, but adds little drama.

EXAMPLE: *Proving agency may be necessary to win your lawsuit, yet it is a boring process that does not impress jurors. You do not want to spend time on a concept that suggests one person should be responsible for the conduct of another person.*

If you cannot use stipulation, do not try to prove agency through the agent, or through circumstances that require time. Ask for permission and then read to the jury from the interrogatories:

"Question 1. On January 6th, 1984 was John Jones employed by your company?"

"Yes."

"Question 2. On that date was he driving a truck owned by your company, delivering merchandise as part of that employment?"

"Yes."

"Question 3. Was that the accident in which plaintiff was injured?"

"Yes."

CONCLUSION

Every word of your dialogue must take you one step closer to winning your lawsuit. If you lose your audience, you may lose your lawsuit.

KEEPING ANY AUDIENCE ON YOUR SIDE THROUGH THE TRIAL

1. Let the jurors know you are helping them perform their duty.
2. Make everything as clever as possible, and jurors will appreciate your effort.
3. Proceed effectively and professionally.
4. Let jurors know you want to win and expect to win.

CREATE BELIEVABLE WITNESSES WITH DIALOGUE

You may not be able to "choose" your "cast," but you can develop those characters who are the witnesses in your courtroom drama so they portray your client's cause in its most favorable light. You can do this through the proper use of dialogue.

Develop Character with Dialogue

Clarence Darrow once said that no jury will send a man to prison if he is liked. It is your job to make the jury like your client, whether it is a criminal or civil trial. You can accomplish this by devoting dialogue to the express purpose of making your client look favorable to the jury.

For example, in your opening statement you may introduce your client as the most important person in your drama:

> "Mary Jones is a registered nurse and has been around pain every day for many years. She is the mother of three children, and she has helped those children when they have skinned their knees, cut new teeth, and when one of them broke an arm.
>
> "Mary Jones learned what pain is really all about on New Year's Eve of 1984 when she was struck by a truck while crossing a street. Her pelvic bone was fractured, and that is the bone that holds your legs to the rest of your body."

Develop Character of a Party Through Testimony of Other Witnesses

Develop your client as the leading character through the testimony of other witnesses, as well as through his or her own testimony. Tell the jury about your client during *voir dire*, your opening statement, and through the questions you ask. You also will find that third-person witnesses can say nice things about your client that can only be said through a third person. "He is a great guy" sounds much better than "I am a great guy."

EXAMPLE: CHARACTER DEVELOPMENT THROUGH PERSONAL TESTIMONY

"How old are you?"
     "Eighty-two years old."
     "I believe you live in the house that we have been talking about in this lawsuit, is that right?"
     "Yes."

"Will you describe that home to the Court?"

"It is a small home that has a nice flower garden."

"Do you raise flowers?"

"Yes."

"Do you sell flowers?"

"Oh, no. I give them to friends and take them to church. I think a church should have flowers in it."

"Your daughter has charged that you are too generous with your church. How much do you contribute?"

"About five dollars a week. I wish I could give more, but I just can't afford to."

"I notice that you speak with an accent, were you born in this country?"

"No. I came from Germany when I was a little girl. I could not speak any English. (Laughing) I hope by now I can talk so you can understand me."

Everyone in the courtroom smiles.

"Yes, Mrs. Schmidt, we can understand you. Now, in this lawsuit you have filed a lawsuit against your daughter, is that right?"

"Yes, I didn't want to, but she is taking my home from me, and that is all I have in the world. I don't know where I would live."

"Before you filed this lawsuit, did you talk with your daughter?"

"Yes, several times. Then I had you write a letter to her, and she just won't give me my home. I didn't want to sue her, but what could I do?"

Very little of that dialogue proves any issue in the lawsuit, yet it is extremely important. It develops character! By the end of the trial word had spread throughout the courthouse about this elderly woman who was being taken advantage of by her own daughter. People would come up to her in the hallway and wish her well.

The judge ordered the daughter to deed the property back to the mother, and the Missouri Court of Appeals affirmed "the sound discretion of the trial court."

CONCLUSION

We are not given a cast of professional actors in the courtroom. The timid amateurs we put on the witness stand to tell our story need the best dialogue we can give them. Listen to witnesses as you interview them. Use their words, and let the dialogue from that interview flow from the witness stand.

HOW TO QUESTION WITNESSES BEFORE TRIAL
TO GET THE MOST DRAMATIC IMPACT AT THE TRIAL

1. Look for the kind of words the witness uses and determine how you can lead into the witness's best words.
2. Determine how many yes and no answers you should use with each witness and how much narrative will be effective.
3. Teach the witness, but determine early in the conference how much learning the witness is capable of.
4. Explain to the witness what you are trying to accomplish and ask for support in your cause.
5. Remember, the witness will probably not feel comfortable in the courtroom and will appreciate your help.

CREATE ATMOSPHERE

Trial lawyers must know how to create atmosphere with dialogue. This process can begin with the *voir dire*. For example:

> "Some of you may remember the night of the big storm last winter, when the power lines were down in most of the city. Well, on that night Marilyn Williams was standing on the curb, in that cold and snow, waiting for her husband to bring the car when a drunk ran onto the curb and struck her. There was a small article in the newspaper about this. Did any of you read that article or in any other way know of this incident?"

Plaintiff's attorney is the first person to address the jury, and he or she has a right to find out whether or not prospective jurors know anything about the case they are about to hear. This enables you to start the trial with the kind of dialogue that will create drama within the courtroom.

Make the Atmosphere Match the Seriousness of Your Dominant Theme

There is always a dominant theme in a trial, and usually that theme is a very serious one. Whether a person goes to prison, who gets custody of the children, or whether someone receives or pays a huge sum of money are all serious issues. The dominant atmosphere must match the dominant theme.

The first words spoken during *voir dire* should create the mood that matches the theme. By the end of the opening statement, the atmosphere should be felt throughout the courtroom. The atmosphere cannot be maintained with the same intensity throughout the trial, and it is a mistake to attempt to do so. Knowing when we can blend various emotions is a part of recognizing the proper atmosphere. For example: counsel began his *voir dire* as follows:

"On July 4th of last year, Mr. Smith, here at the counsel table, was attending a family picnic at Chain-of-Rocks Park. Is there anyone who does not know where this park is located?

"While the children took a ride in a horse-drawn wagon, the men pitched horseshoes. When Mr. Smith heard the children screaming he noticed the driver had lost control of the wagon and he rushed to try to stop the wagon. Have any of you read about this incident in the newspapers?

"The screaming of the children stopped as Mr. Smith stopped the wagon, but Mr. Smith's leg got caught under the wheel of the wagon. At the close of the trial, his Honor will instruct you as to the law of our state as it is to be applied to this lawsuit. But with this little information I have given you, is there anyone on this jury panel who has already formed an opinion as to whether or not the owner of the amusement park should be held responsible for the injuries sustained by Mr. Smith?

"Our evidence will show the ligaments in Mr. Smith's leg were turned and torn and that his use of that leg will be extremely limited, so I will be asking for a substantial verdict. Now, are you willing to wait and listen to all of the evidence before forming an opinion as to damages, or any other issue in this case?"

Phrases such as "family picnic," "children screaming," "lost control," "leg caught under the wheel," "responsible for injuries," and "turned and torn" help create atmosphere. Use them!

CONCLUSION

You have days in which you want to be real nice to everyone in the world, and you probably have days when you are not quite so charitable. People who serve on juries have "moods" that have a direct bearing on how charitable they will be with your client. Your dialogue can create the atmosphere that will put them in the mood most favorable to your client.

USE WORDS THAT CAN MOVE A JURY TO YOUR SIDE

1. Use words that create an image of what you wish to convey; and
2. Prepare for words that will not present your client's cause in a favorable light.

ADVANCE THE PLOT OF YOUR DRAMA

Most dialogue of a play is for the purpose of advancing the plot. Dialogue for this specific purpose should also be an important part of your courtroom drama.

Tell Your Story with Good Dialogue

The jury should always be conscious of where the story is going. This can best be accomplished by making the story move toward the goal at a rapid and interesting pace. Jurors will listen to testimony that moves.

Telling your story by advancing the plot is what the trial is all about. Everything else is ancillary to that. If you don't tell your story fully enough, you won't prove your case so you won't get to the jury. If you don't tell your story effectively enough, it won't do you any good to get to the jury.

Make Your Story Move Rapidly

People who sit on the jury expect to be fed the story in capsule form. They know nothing of your having to make a full and complete record, so even your most tedious task should be stepped up. If your story does not move, it will not sell.

Give your case the dialogue it needs to tell the story. From *voir dire* through final argument, you are the chief spokesman for your client, and you must communicate the message.

EXAMPLE: TELLING YOUR CLIENT'S STORY AS QUICKLY AS POSSIBLE

Through my client's testimony, we established some question as to the validity of a will. By reading into evidence from the depositions of the witnesses to the will, we increased the suspicion. The scene was then set for the dialogue that advanced the plot and eventually led to the kind of fee I dreamed of in law school.

> "When did you retire and move to Florida?"
> "About two years ago."
> "By whom were you employed before your retirement?"
> "The Army Intelligence."
> "In what capacity?"
> "As an examiner of questioned documents."

"How long did you serve that branch of the Army in that capacity?"

"About twenty-three years."

At this point, opposing counsel stipulated as to the expert's qualifications, and we proceeded with the dialogue.

"Do you remember meeting me at the county courthouse last spring?"

"Yes."

"On that day, did you and I go to the Probate Division of the Circuit Court?"

"Yes."

"At that time, did I deliver to you certain documents?"

"Yes."

"Had you requested these documents?"

"Yes."

"What were the documents?"

"They consisted of correspondence, deeds, and other papers containing the signature of the deceased."

"Did you examine these papers?"

"Yes."

"For what purpose?"

"To obtain a sampling of the deceased's signature."

"Did you examine any other documents on that date?"

"Yes. I examined the will of the deceased that was admitted to probate in this estate."

"Did you examine the signature on that will?"

"Yes."

"Did you compare that signature with the signature of the deceased on the other documents that were signed by the deceased?"

"Yes."

"What did you find?"

"I found that the will had been signed by one person, and all of the other documents had been signed by another person."

"Over what period of time were these other documents executed?"

"Over a period of several years."

"You testified that among those documents were letters written by the deceased, were those letters type-written and signed by the deceased, or were the entire letters handwritten?"

"The entire letters were handwritten."

"Over what period of time were these letters written?"

"Over a period of several years."

"You mentioned a deed; what was that document?"

"A deed deceased and her husband had executed a number of years ago. It had been recorded as an official document."

"I am now referring to the documents, other than the will admitted to probate in this estate. Did you find any reason to question the validity of the signature on those documents?"

"No, I did not."

"Based on your examination of those documents, and your examination of the will admitted to probate in this estate, do you have an opinion, based on a reasonable degree of certainty, and based on your training and experience in your chosen field as an examiner of questioned documents, as to the validity of the signature on the will admitted to probate in this estate?"

"Yes."

"What is that opinion?"

"The signature on the will admitted to probate in this estate is not that of the deceased. It is a forgery."

We could have reached that final, magic sentence with fewer words, but each scene has its own requirements. When you are calling someone a liar, or showing that person guilty of such antisocial conduct as forgery, that person is entitled to a certain degree of thoroughness. Besides, when you have an excellent witness on the stand who is giving testimony devastating to the opposition, you should keep that witness center stage long enough for his or her presence to be fully appreciated.

ALTERNATE STRATEGY: *Some lawyers refuse to waive the expert's qualifications. This trial was in Florida, where will con-*

tests are tried before the judge. Had the trial been in Missouri, where such cases are tried before a jury, I may not have permitted a waiver, and would have insisted on the expert telling the jury all of his qualifications. Notice that the judge is interested in qualifications, but once you have made your point with the judge, you can stop a little sooner.

CONCLUSION

Advancing the plot is the only aspect of the trial that directly tells your story. Other aspects are important, but never forget why you are in that courtroom. You are there to tell your client's story and you must move toward that goal as swiftly as possible.

METHODS TO MOVE YOUR DRAMA

1. Outline what you must prove, and prove it.
2. Use a "cumulative" witness only when the added impact outweighs the time invested in the testimony.
3. Move through "mechanics of proof" as rapidly as possible by pre-marking exhibits, stipulating to the unimportant, and other time-saving steps.
4. Make every word count.

WORDS ARE THE TOOLS OF YOUR TRADE— USE THEM

Most of your story will be told with words. Your choice of words is important, so you must find which words will help you win your lawsuit.

Choose Words That Have a Dramatic Impact

Nearly all of the evidence you will introduce will be oral testimony, and when you address the jury as a spokesperson for your client, you will use words, the tools of your trade.

Trial lawyers who have an interest in words should develop that interest by reading such books as Professor Strunk's, *The Elements of Style*, as updated by his student, E. B. White. This small paperback can be carried in your suitcoat pocket and can be read one page at a time.

Professor Strunk's book has been described as "an attempt to cut the vast tangle of English rhetoric down to size." "Omit needless words!" was not a suggestion but a command from the professor that every juror wants every lawyer to heed. When the professor made such suggestions as "Do not overstate," "Do not explain too much," and "Avoid fancy words," he might have had trial lawyers in mind.

Develop Pride in Your Use and Non-Use of Words

There are classic uses and misuses of certain words by trial lawyers. In a personal injury case, the defense lawyer talks about an "accident," since accidents "just happen," and the word does not suggest that someone caused it to happen. The plaintiff's attorney will speak of a "collision" in which the defendant collided with plaintiff, suggesting blame. The plaintiff's attorney may talk of a child going in front of a fast-moving car, but the defendant's lawyer will talk about the child "darting" in front of a car (see Figure 8-2).

Some words are too powerful. Don't suggest that anyone is a liar, unless you are sure the jury is ready for this severe treatment of a fellow human being. Even if you prove that a witness or a party is a liar, you usually are wise to let the jury do the labelling.

In one case, I found that the jury did not like to hear the word "cancer." They were impressed by testimony relating to the subject, but I sensed a definite feeling among the jurors that they would just as soon not hear that word. However, in a different kind of case, the way the word is presented may have a different effect. Since it is a dreaded word, an attorney may want to use it and the power it portrays. Weigh all circumstances and keep a close eye on the jury— and remember that although jurors are impressed with powerful words, there are words that make them feel uncomfortable.

Figure 8-1   VERY-ABLES

MAKE A LIST OF "VERY-ABLES," IT WILL HELP YOU TO
REMEMBER!

Instead of *"very* interesting," WHY NOT *"fascinating"*?

Instead of *"very* smart," WHY NOT *"brilliant"*?

Instead of *"very* large," WHY NOT *"huge"*?

Instead of *"very* bad," WHY NOT *"horrible"*?

Instead of *"very* unimportant," WHY NOT *"insignificant"*?

STRONG WORDS MAKE A MORE FORCEFUL LANGUAGE!

Figure 8-2   Plaintiff-Defendant Words

Words Attorneys for Plaintiffs-Defendants Use

Plaintiff	Defendant
Collision	Accident
Defendant	Harry
Bobby	Plaintiff

Both Attorneys

Auto or car	NOT	Motor Vehicle
Drove	NOT	Operated
Before	NOT	Prior To
After	NOT	Subsequent To

Avoid Words That Have a Negative Effect

Some words are simply to be avoided. Many women prefer "Ms.," but I also find women who are offended by its use. "Housewife" is alright, but "just a housewife" can be fatal during *voir dire*. Steer clear of racist, sexist cliches—your client deserves better.

EXAMPLE: USING WORDS THE JURY CAN RELATE TO

"Now tell me, Officer, when this man cursed you, you got mad, didn't you?"

"Of course, I got mad, wouldn't you?"

"And when you got mad, you didn't just stand there and do nothing, did you?"

"What do you mean?"

"I mean you did something, didn't you?"

"No. I didn't strike him."

"Did you touch him?"

"I grabbed him."

"Was he escaping from you?"

"No."

"Was he coming toward you?"

"No."

"In fact, he was just standing there, wasn't he?"

"Yes, I guess so."

"You didn't grab him because he was escaping or coming at you. You grabbed him because you were mad, isn't that right?"

"I told you I was mad."

"Did you immediately let go of him?"

"Not immediately."

"Did you hold him tightly enough so that he could not escape or come at you?"

"Yes."

"Did he at any time try to escape, or come at you?"

"No."

"Then this force you were using was because you were mad, not because it was required for any professional law enforcement purpose, is that not true?"

Opposing counsel objected, but by then the officer had pretty well committed himself.

One day I sat in a courtroom waiting my turn on a non-contested divorce matter. An attorney approached the witness stand and handed the witness a piece of paper.

"I have just handed you what has been marked Petitioner's exhibit 1. Do you recognize this exhibit?"

"Yes."

"What does it purport to be?"

"I don't know."

"What do you mean, you don't know?" the lawyer said with a bewildered look on his face.

"I mean I don't know."

"You signed this piece of paper, did you not?"

"Yes."

"And, you don't know what it is?"

"Oh, you want to know what this piece of paper is. It is the property settlement my husband and I signed."

As I sat in the courtroom, I realized that I had followed a somewhat similar procedure since my first year in practice, when I saw that was how the "older lawyers" did it. I also realized that I had never used the word purport outside the courtroom. Since that day, I have used a more practical approach:

"I show you what has been marked Petitioner's Exhibit 1, do you recognize it?"

"Yes."

"Do you know what it is?"

"Yes."

"What is it?"

"It is the property settlement my husband and I signed."

CONCLUSION

Words still are our most basic means of communicating our thoughts. Once you have decided to win, you have decided to use the best words you can find. Those are words that the jury will understand, those with which they can identify, and those that will move the jury toward your client's position in the lawsuit.

A FEW BASICS FOR COMMUNICATING TO WIN

1. Use words that dramatize your story.
2. Use words with which the jury can identify.
3. Use words that the jury can understand.
4. Use words that move the jury toward your client's position.

DECIDE WHICH CHARACTERS
DESERVE WHAT DIALOGUE

Early in the planning of your courtroom drama, you must decide a crucial question: Which of your witnesses will tell which part of your story?

Decide Who Will Tell What in Your Drama

Every lawyer is called upon to make the same decision—that is, whether your story will be told in first person, or by other witnesses. You must decide at the outset, which witnesses, through testimony, will describe various scenes of your courtroom drama.

A story can be told by either of two witnesses. Choose the right witness. If a husband and wife had a conference with the realtor in a suit over a sales contract, don't assume you will put the husband on first. Size up the two witnesses. Have the best witness tell the story and have the other witness confirm that testimony and fill in the details. Keep your eye on the jury, however, because the makeup of the jury may help you decide which witness to use first.

For example, a young man was truly being tried by his peers, as nearly all of the jurors were of his approximate age. Counsel called him as the first witness for the defense. Had the jury members been older, counsel would have called the school teacher witness first to give the defendant credibility before taking the stand.

Avoid the Horrors of Too Many Witnesses Telling the Same Story

If you have two witnesses and one will be a terrible witness, send the terrible witness home. Get this witness out of the courtroom before opposing counsel calls that witness to the stand. You do not need two witnesses to tell the same story, especially since they may not tell it the same way.

When I started practicing law in 1950, the rule as to separation of witnesses was basically restricted to criminal cases, but today I find an extensive use of the rule in civil cases.

Let Others Tell How Good Your Expert Is

When using expert witnesses, plan an introduction. It is awkward for Dr. Smith to say, "I am the greatest authority in the world." It may be better for Dr. Jones to say, "I referred the patient to Dr. Smith, because he is the greatest authority in the world," or to have the boy's mother say, "I wanted the very best for my son and went to Dr. Smith, because he is the greatest authority in the world." (Evidentuary problem? If so, then lay the foundation yourself and make it abundantly clear that Dr. Smith is the greatest authority in the world.)

Jurors Want to Hear Your Client

Use a supporting cast, but remember that you and your client are the most important people of your drama. Save yourself some good lines, because the jury will expect that of you. Feed some good lines to your client, because the jury is anxious to hear the client tell his or her story.

In a criminal case, the jury always wants to hear your client. If you are able to put your client on the stand, end his or her testimony something like this:

> "John, were you on Mr. Brown's property that night?"
> "No."
> "Have you ever been on Mr. Brown's property?"
> "No."
> "Do you know where Mr. Brown's property is?"
> "I do now."
> "Did you on the night in question?"
> "No."
> "Did you ever break into Mr. Brown's home, or any other home, in your entire life?"
> "Absolutely not."

Don't deny your client this opportunity! Don't deny the jury of the opportunity to hear him say he is innocent.

Tell Your Story with More Than Testimony

All of the story need not be told through testimony. Use dialogue during *voir dire* and opening statement that will set the scene for your supporting cast.

EXAMPLE: SETTING THE SCENE DURING VOIR DIRE

> "Mary Smith is a secretary, and since her husband, John, works in construction, he is home when she arrives from the office. On the night of September 14th, 1984 John was not home, because he had gone to K-Mart to buy Mary a present and was falsely arrested and was sitting in jail while Mary was desperately looking for him."
> "Do any of you know anything about this incident?"

EXAMPLE: *SETTING THE SCENE DURING OPENING STATEMENT*

"John Smith had never received as much as a traffic ticket and on September 14th, he went to K-Mart for one reason, to buy his wife a present. Because the security at K-Mart thought John looked like someone who had been shoplifting in their store, they had him arrested, and he spent five hours sitting in jail, with a convicted rapist on one side of him and the town drunk on the other side of him.

Much of your story can be told by witnesses close to the client's spouse, a close friend, or the boss at work. They often are your best witnesses.

EXAMPLE: *CHOOSING WITNESSES WHO WILL HELP YOUR DRAMA*

"Did you visit your wife while she was in the hospital?"
"Yes."
"Did you visit her while she was in intensive care?"
"Yes."
"How long was she in intensive care?"
"Two weeks."
"When you visited her in intensive care, did you talk with her?"
"No. Most of the time she was not conscious. She would come to for a few minutes and would look at me, but would say nothing."
"Did you talk with her?"
"Yes. I tried, but it was like she couldn't understand what I was saying."
"What, if anything, did you observe about her at this time."
"She had pained expressions on her face."
"Did you visit her after she left the intensive care unit?"
"Yes. She was in the hospital for another two months."

"Did you notice anything unusual about her during this period of time."

"Yes. Up to the last week, she had a cast from her waist to her feet."

"How often did you visit her?"

"I went there every day after work and stayed until visiting hours were over at eight."

"What did you and your wife do during those hours?"

"Most of the time she slept, but when she was awake we talked and I watched the nurse take care of her."

"What did the nurse do while you were there?"

"Moved her to different positions and gave her drugs."

"Do you know, of your own knowledge, what kind of drugs?"

"A lot of pain killers, I know that."

"When she came home, who performed the usual household duties?"

"I did, for about six months."

Much of this could have been testified to by the wife, without this testimony from the husband. This kind of evidence, however, can be very effective if it comes from a second or third person, such as a spouse or fellow worker. When the foreman at the plant says, "Nell just isn't the same person she was before the accident," it means much more than testimony from the plaintiff, which is always subject to suspicion.

CONCLUSION

Once you have chosen the dialogue that will win your lawsuit, you must then decide from whom this dialogue will come. You and your witnesses, and even opposing counsel's witnesses, are among the members of the cast who can deliver those magic words. Choose your spokesperson wisely.

Use opposing counsel's witnesses, including his or her own client, live or by deposition. You don't have to wait for cross-examination. During plaintiff's case, you can read to the jury from the defendant's deposition. "I had too much to drink, I just didn't see the kid."

**THE KIND OF DIALOGUE THAT WILL WIN
YOUR LAWSUIT AND HOW YOU GET YOUR WITNESSES
TO SAY WHAT YOU WANT**

1. While reviewing with a witness what the witness will say, also discuss how it should be said.
2. Use dialogue at a time in the trial when it will have its most dramatic impact.
3. Decide in advance of trial, which dialogue will be most effective if it comes during *voir dire*, opening statement, direct examination, cross examination, or final argument.
4. Use leading questions during interview, obtain the proper response, then use non-leading questions in the courtroom and have the witness give the words you had suggested during the interview, providing you get the proper response to the leading questions. (If you say "The light was red, wasn't it?" you are likely to get a response that the light was red, even if you know the light was green and the witness thought the light was green, so there is nothing wrong with saying, "Our investigation shows the light was green. What do you remember?")

KEEP THE DIALOGUE CRISP

You will look sharp, and you will be sharp, if you tell your story with sharp dialogue. Good crisp, sharp dialogue is what makes a drama move, and it enables the audience to enjoy drama. This can help you win your lawsuit!

EXAMPLE: CRISP DIALOGUE MAKES YOUR DRAMA MOVE

Defending a woman whose car has had contact with a child is difficult, and a situation in which the defendant's case should be stated briefly and convincingly. To have the defendant discuss it in much detail would seem to some jurors to be the making of excuses. That is why counsel moves swiftly through the scene with crisp dialogue:

"When did you first see the boy?"
"When he darted from behind the car."
"What did you do?"
"I slammed on my brakes."
"What did the boy do?"
"He ran into the side of my car."

Be "Quotable," and the Jury Will Remember
Your Words While Deliberating

Will the jury quote you while deliberating? That may well depend
on how "quotable" you are. People only quote what is easy to quote
and easy to remember.

For example, when the judgment is for $50,000 in principal and
$6,112.16 in interest, tell the jury, "Your verdict should be in the
sum of $50,000 in principal and $6,000 in interest." By waiving a few
dollars in interest, the jury will be able to "quote" you easily in the
precise sum of $56,000 and that will probably be the amount of the
verdict.

The jury will not remember all you, or your witnesses, say, but
they will remember key words, phrases, and sentences. You want
someone on that jury to suggest during the deliberation. "You know,
that officer got mad and that's why he grabbed this man." Being
quoted in the jury room is the dream of every good trial lawyer, and
the result of good, crisp dialogue.

EXAMPLE: SELECTING DIALOGUE THAT'S
BRIEF BUT STRONG

*Some of my favorite dialogue comes from my days as a city
prosecutor, probably because of the succinctness of this form of
drama. One police report told the whole story with this brief entry:
"Willie was stopped by the officer. Willie cursed the officer. Willie
was taken to the County Hospital."*

*Only once during my entire career did I prosecute a woman for
indecent exposure. The dialogue went something like this:*

"What were you wearing when the officer stopped you
in the middle of Carson Road?"
"This little blouse I am wearing tonight."

"What else were you wearing?"
"Nothing."

I later learned the young lady was practicing her trade in the back seat of an automobile on the main street in town, when an inquisitive officer intruded with his flashlight. The young lady jumped from the car and ran down the street in her flimsly little blouse, right into the arms of the law.

In another case, an elderly woman complained that the young woman who rented the apartment above her was operating a house of ill fame. The young woman testified in her own defense, and she was a little spitfire.

"Is it not true that at 10:00 P.M. on the night in question a man walked up that stairway to your apartment?"

"That is true."

"And half an hour later he came down?"

"Yes. He sure did."

"Then another man walked up that same stairway to your apartment, is that not true?"

"Now, wait a minute, attorney, can I help it if I'm popular?"

The judge will be very patient with you, but he and the jury will appreciate good, crisp dialogue. You are not getting paid by the word.

CONCLUSION

Be brief!

HOW TO MAINTAIN BREVITY

1. Ask questions that will prompt brief answers.
2. Caution witnesses before they take the stand that brevity is godliness.
3. Remember that *you* are not being paid by the word.

BUILD CREDIBILITY WITH DIALOGUE

Every word that is uttered in the courtroom will either help or hurt you and bring you one word closer to victory or defeat. That is because each word has some effect upon the jury's believing or disbelieving your story. This is *credibility*, and this is a primary purpose of dialogue.

Establish Your Credibility Through Dialogue

Since lawsuits are being won or lost early in the trial, it is extremely important that dialogue aimed at building credibility should be injected into the lawsuit as soon as possible. Deciding during final argument that you and your client are really good guys may be too late to affect a decision made early in the trial.

EXAMPLE: *You cannot tell the jury in your final argument, "The first thing I told you during voir dire . . . ," unless it was the first thing you said during voir dire. You cannot share your credibility with your client during final argument, with such phrases as "Lou and I," unless you have built from the start a credibility to share. Once you lay that foundation, the final argument will sound sincere and be effective:*

"When you reach age 60, as Lou and I have, there are many things about your body that are not as good as they used to be. We know that. We don't need some lawyer to tell us that. And, we don't need some young lawyer to suggest that we are trying to take advantage of someone because our body is not as good as it used to be.

"The first thing I told you during *voir dire* was that Lou does not want one dime he is not entitled to, but it is my duty to see that Lou *does* get every dime he *is* entitled to, and it is your duty to return a verdict that gives Lou every dime he is entitled to under the evidence of this case, and under the laws of our state.

"This may be the only day in your life when you can show publicly your concern for what has happened to another human being. You should be proud of that concern, and I know you will return a substantial verdict that you will be proud of for the rest of your life."

Dialogue aimed at building credibility must be more than mere words, because credibility is more than a hollow concept or a convenient goal. Credibility must be based on genuine sincerity, and so must the dialogue supporting it. Jurors have the ability to look right through the veneer of artificiality.

Your client can use part of his or her storytelling to build credibility. "I was on the way to a church meeting" may be included, while "I was on the way home from a bar" is just not necessary to your cause.

Other witnesses can do even more to establish your client's credibility. As long as the passenger has to be in court to testify that the light was green, a small amount of additional dialogue will not be costly in time or strategy, so add: "By the way, are you related to my client?" "Oh, no, she has just been a den mother for two of my daughters." You have added another notch to credibility.

Know why you are asking that question! If you ask a single question without a purpose, it may come back to haunt you.

Use Dialogue to Get the Jury to Like Your Client

Credibility is getting the jury to like your client and believe in his or her cause. The fact that she is a den mother may suggest that your client can be believed. It may also suggest that she is a good person who devotes time to girls and the jury may like her for it. Don't worry about distinguishing between credibility and likeableness. They are the two qualities you hope the jury will find in your client, and if they both happen at the same time, that is just fine.

Establish Your Client's Credibility
Through Your Dialogue

The judge will instruct the jury that what you say is not evidence, but every jury will weigh what you say as a true test of your credibility and of your client's credibility. Clients often want you to ask questions for the sole purpose of embarrassing a witness. If you give into this juvenile concept of trial strategy, you are damaging your client's cause.

You eventually will stand before that jury and tell its members what verdict they should return. Every word you speak, even the questions you ask, have been fed subconsciously into the mind of each juror. What you have said, and how you have said it, will have registered more than you might imagine.

EXAMPLE: USING DIALOGUE TO ESTABLISH CREDIBILITY

"We lawyers have filed papers in this lawsuit that we call pleadings. Is there anyone on this jury panel who does not understand that these pleadings are prepared by the lawyers, and not by the clients?"

"I take it from your silence that this is clear to you."

"Among these pleadings that I have filed in this lawsuit for my client, is a paper we call the petition, and in that petition there is a paragraph we call the prayer for damages, which contains a dollar figure, which is the most you can return a verdict for in this lawsuit. Now is there anyone among you who has any doubt in your mind when I tell you that I chose that figure, and put that figure in the petition, and not my client?"

"His Honor has instructed you that what appears in these pleadings, like what we lawyers say, is not evidence, and that your verdict is to be based on the evidence that comes from this witness stand. Please raise your hand if you feel you will have any problem following the court's instruction in that respect?"

"At this stage of the trial, you know nothing about the facts of this case, so I assume you have not formed an opinion as to what the amount of the verdict should be. After you have heard all of the evidence and after you have heard all the argument of both lawyers, you will be able to decide on a verdict amount."

All of this dialogue during voir dire *was for but one purpose: to establish credibility. During my first year in practice, I watched a trial in which a veteran insurance company lawyer crucified a* woman during cross-examination for asking for $100,000 because she had a "sore neck."

As I watched that bewildered witness squirm, I swore I would never place a client in such a position. I try to clear up such matters during voir dire so we can proceed with the real issues of the case.

ALTERNATE STRATEGY: In states that require the dollar figure in the prayer for damages, or where the lawyer chooses to do so though not required, choosing a reasonable sum will avoid this problem. Since it is becoming more important not to place too low a ceiling on your prayer, another strategy is to sue for the huge amount, but make everything at the trial cause the jury to accept that amount as not being reasonable.

CONCLUSION

Dialogue is the means with which you unfold your drama, and an important part of that dialogue must be aimed at establishing credibility. Every word you speak during voir dire, examining witnesses, or argument, gives the jury some hint as to whether or not to believe you. The words your witnesses speak greatly affect their credibility. You do have a responsibility for those words. You don't just wind up a witness like a toy and absolve yourself from the chatter that is bound to flow from it.

HOW CREDIBILITY CAN BE USED TO MAXIMIZE YOUR DRAMA

1. Review with a witness the content of the testimony, and strike that which will hurt the credibility of the witness, if possible.
2. Make sure you and your witnesses use words that project sincerity.
3. Make sure you and your witnesses conduct yourselves throughout the trial in a manner consistent with all else that is happening during the trial.

CHAPTER NINE

Believe and You Will Cause Others to Believe

MAKE SURE YOUR STORY IS BELIEVABLE

When the Broadway critic sits with pad in hand on opening night, he is asking himself, "Is the story believable?" The jury is asking the same question. Nothing will sell if your story does not sell.

Analyze Your Story to Appraise Believability

Try hard to look at your story with a professional detachment. If that is not possible, tell the story to others and let them pick it apart. Do not start down the road to trial until you have properly appraised your story from the standpoint of believability.

If You Have a Choice of Theories, Choose the One That Is Believable

You can repair believability shortcomings by choosing the most believable of alternative theories or by emphasizing the most believable parts of the story. You have enjoyed plays that have had weaknesses, and juries have returned favorable verdicts in cases that have had weaknesses.

Tell Your Story in a Believable Way

When a little girl tells you that she has not been in the cookie jar, you usually can tell right away whether or not you believe her. Your decision is not based on the story that is being told, but on the *way* the story is told. The tone of her voice, whether she is looking at the floor or at you, and whether she is "protesting too much" are factors that render much or little credence to her story.

Believability Is a Part of Drama

For drama to be effective, it must be believable. A dramatic appeal suggests that you are appealing to emotion and not reason. However, if your drama is believable, the drama reinforces reason and gives jurors a chance to join your cause with their minds as well as their hearts.

Credibility Is a Part of Drama

When a trial lawyer is dramatic, he is laying his credibility on the line. In doing so, he assumes great risk if he appears insincere, is putting on a show, or is presenting an argument that is unbelievable. Credibility is what a lawsuit is all about, and drama magnifies the credibility factor—so it is imperative that the trial lawyer proceed on the firm ground of believability.

If Your Story Is Unbelievable Beyond Salvation, Junk It

When you are stuck with a story you can't sell—settle, cop a plea, or just get out! Maybe someone else can sell it. Be honest with yourself and with your client when you face up to a story that is simply not believable!

EXAMPLE: EXAMINING YOUR CLIENT'S STORY FOR BELIEVABILITY

Two young men, age eighteen, black, unemployed, school dropouts, one with a criminal record, were driving through a residential neighborhood at eleven o'clock in the morning. The driver stopped the car and the passenger got out. The driver then proceeded to drive around the block and returned to the place where he had left off the passenger.

The passenger jumped into the car and the two young men took off to a favorite restaurant where they began to eat a sandwich. Within a few minutes, an officer apprehended them at the restaurant and took them to the station and booked them for burglary.

The passenger pleaded guilty to breaking into a home, and taking some jewelry and a few dollars in cash. The driver insisted he had no idea the passenger was going to burglarize the home. He claimed that the other young man told him he wanted to talk to a girlfriend for a minute and to drive around the block once and pick him up.

The passenger had pleaded guilty to a previous burglary and the driver knew this, but the driver had no criminal record. The driver retains you to represent him. Do you believe his story?

You may have serious doubts about the story, and there is nothing wrong with that. You should honestly appraise your client's story. Give yourself the benefit of your gut reaction. Do not "convict" your client, even in your own mind, but face the case realistically.

Ask questions! Your first question should be "Why did you drive around the block, rather than pull over and wait for your friend?" The prosecutor is going to ask that question and even suggest to the jury the reason was that he did not want neighbors to identify the car.

The driver protested his innocence, but two days before a jury trial, he admitted he was guilty and wanted to change his plea. The morning of trial, however, he told his aunt in his attorney's presence that he was really innocent, but the lawyer told him to plead guilty.

Counsel asked him, "Do you see that door to that courtroom?"

"Yes."

"Well, in about two minutes you and I are going to walk through that door into that courtroom, and we are going to approach the bench and tell the judge that you are not guilty, and that you want a jury of twelve citizens to hear your case."

The young man thought about that for a moment, then admitted to his aunt that he was guilty, that counsel had advised him of his rights, and that he wanted nothing to do with going before that jury. If a client's case is not believable, he is not interested in "justice" as provided for him in the constitution.

CONCLUSION

Your story is what you are selling to the jury. Make sure it is something you can sell. Examine your story carefully and realize the more you believe the story, the better your chances are that the jury will believe it.

**WHAT TO LOOK FOR TO DEVELOP YOUR CONFIDENCE
'IN YOUR DRAMA**

1. Think twice before accepting a lawsuit that you really don't believe in.
2. If you have a choice of theories, choose the one you feel most comfortable with, if this is consistent with your client's goal.
3. Get involved with the human aspects of your lawsuit, so that by the time you walk into the courtroom you really want to win!

HELP YOUR CHARACTERS
CONVINCE THE AUDIENCE

Once the attorney has decided that the story is believable, the question is then asked: "Is the story told through characters that are believable?" You must get the story from your file to the jury through the characters you put on the stage. Whether the jury returns a favorable verdict will much depend upon the believability of those witnesses.

Analyze Your Witnesses as to Believability

Oral testimony is necessary to establish your case. It enables you to "get to the jury." Once you reach the jury, however, your effort is for naught unless the jury believes the testimony.

Who testified is important! *How* that witness testified is important! *What* that witness said is important! Plan your oral testimony with believability in mind!

Try to Avoid Use of Characters
Who Are Not Believable

If a witness is going to hurt you, make sure you can't establish his or her proof through another witness or other means. If you must use this witness, prepare the jury for him or her.

Much testimony is cumulative, and using a poor witness for that purpose is a common mistake. If any witness is not going to help you, why use him or her? If you know he or she is a risk, certainly don't use him or her unless absolutely necessary.

Present Believability of Your Witnesses
in a Positive Way

Present all of your characters in a positive manner. People are more apt to believe a person they know and a person they like. A playwright introduces his or her audience to a character before asking it to believe that character. If a playwright wants the audience to disbelieve a character, he or she may introduce that character in a negative way.

If through *voir dire* and opening statement, and even through the testimony of other witnesses, the jury is familiar with a witness, it may be ready to accept his or her testimony. When you represent the plaintiff, opposing counsel has little chance to offset this before the witness testifies.

EXAMPLE: PREPARING THE JURY
FOR YOUR WITNESSES

During the voir dire:

> "Do any of you know this young man sitting behind me at the counsel table? Larry Evans lives on Magnolia, and works at the brewery."
>
> "Larry lives with his father, John Evans, who runs the grocery store at Park and Magnolia. Have any of you been in that grocery store?"
>
> "When Larry was 18 years old, he got into some trouble with some other young men, but since then he has led a perfect life and has been a real credit to his family and his community. Are you able to judge this case on what Larry did or did not do on July 1 of this year, and not on some stupid mistake he made ten years ago?"

During opening statement:

> "Our evidence will show that when Larry walked into that tavern he did not know his friend was carrying a gun. Eyewitnesses will testify that there was no gun within

view of anyone until this other man pulled a gun and showed it to the bartender. The bartender will testify that when the other man ran, Larry just stood there for a minute, then went out to get into his car."

During cross-examination:

"Officer, where was Williams when he was apprehended?"

"About a block from the tavern."

"And where was Larry?"

"Outside the tavern, next to his car."

"Did you arrest Larry?"

"Yes."

"Did he give you any trouble?"

"No."

"Did you ask him questions about this incident?"

"Yes."

"Did he answer those questions?"

"Yes."

"Did he, at any time, during this questioning say anything to indicate that he might have known that Williams had a gun?"

"No. He did not."

"How long have you been on the force?"

"Eight years."

"And you are assigned to the district in which Larry lives, is that right?"

"Yes."

"It is not unusual for young men in this neighborhood to have problems with the law, is it, Officer?"

"No. It sure isn't."

"Up to the night in question, did you have *any* problem with Larry?"

"No. Not at all."

We are now ready for Larry to testify. He and the jury have been introduced to each other.

CONCLUSION

Let the jury know your characters before they testify. Prepare the jury for the good and bad believability aspects of a witness. Treat the witnesses as though you believe them, if you expect the jury to believe them.

REMEMBER HOW TO PRESENT THE GOOD AND BAD TO YOUR BEST ADVANTAGE

1. Prepare jurors for the bad aspects of your case by letting them know it is there and convincing them it is not important.
2. Identify the best aspects of your case and dramatize them from the start.
3. Tell the jury what is important and explain why opposing counsel dwells on the unimportant.
4. Emphasize the unfairness of other party dwelling on an unimportant aspect that is a weakness of your case.

ESTABLISH YOUR OWN CREDIBILITY

You are the central figure in the telling of your story. If you do not believe the story, the jury is likely to recognize this. The degree to which the jury believes is closely aligned with the degree to which you believe.

Try to Avoid Situations in Which You Are Asking the Jury To Believe That Which You Do Not Believe

Most insurance company lawyers I know actually believe that injured people are out to "get" their company, and most plaintiffs' attorneys I know feel very strongly that their clients deserve every dime they get. Most prosecutors I know want to send people to prison, and most defense attorneys in criminal cases feel there is absolutely no value in sending their clients to prison.

That is as it should be! A few lawyers are capable of turning a feeling on and off, but most of us feel with such sincerity that it is best for our client that we really believe what we are saying. If you really believe in your cause, you can be comfortable throughout the trial without having to guard against any word or act that may betray your client's cause.

A friend once was embarrassed by making an ethnic remark in front of a friend. I offered a very simple solution: "Don't make ethnic remarks, and the best way to accomplish that is also very simple— don't think like a bigot."

When an attorney simply does not believe in his cause, he and his client should have a serious discussion. The attorney may become more convinced of his case, the client may become more convinced that settlement possibilities should be pursued, or they may both become convinced that the client should seek other counsel.

This is not to say that lawyers do not or should not represent causes or people with whom they cannot identify. This is especially true in criminal cases, where the right to counsel would be meaningless if such an approach to trials were followed.

Prepare Yourself for Trial by Convincing Yourself of the Validity of Your Case

The courtroom is *not* a stage for the playing of games. The trial of a lawsuit is serious business and demands of us a serious and sincere approach.

Prepare for trial by getting to know your client and his or her cause. If your client believes in his or her case, there must be some reason. Make sure you are not missing something. You will bring your own philosophy and background into a case, but don't let that prejudice your client.

Let the Jury Know You Believe in Your Cause

Don't hesitate to tell the jury that you believe in your client's cause. "I sincerely believe this woman is entitled to a verdict in the sum of $1 million." "You heard Jim when he testified; he sat right there and told you the truth. He told you exactly what happened that night." Think about your client's cause from the moment you are retained and throughout the trial, even during recess.

Charles M. Shaw, the criminal lawyer, spends much of his time devastating police officers in the courtroom, and he once said, "If my best friend were a police officer and came up to me in the hallway during recess, I wouldn't even talk to him. Why, if a juror saw me being friendly with an officer, he'd think I was playing some kind of game in the courtroom."

In a civil action, the plaintiff's attorney has the first opportunity to address the jury, during *voir dire*. Use that opportunity to establish your own credibility! Let the jury know that you care about them, and about your client.

EXAMPLE: MAINTAINING YOUR CREDIBILITY WITH THE JURY

"Is there anyone on this jury panel who just doesn't want to serve on the jury in this case?"

"I don't."

"Why is it you don't want to serve?"

"I served on a jury last year and the lawyers wasted four days on a case that could have been settled, and was settled while we were deliberating. I'm still disgusted and don't want to serve again."

"You seem genuinely concerned, Mrs. Brown, and I gather you have very strong feelings on the subject. Do you think this feeling would keep you from bringing back a verdict that is fair and just to both sides?"

"Yes, I do."

"Your Honor, I feel Mrs. Brown should be excused."

"Your Honor, I object . . ."

"Mrs. Brown, you are excused, and will report to the jury assembly room."

Counsel then turned to the jury and said, "Now, I can't promise results like that if any of you want off the jury, but do any of you want to be excused, for any reason? If so, raise your hand, and we will talk about it."

When no one raised a hand, counsel turned to a mother on the jury and said:

"Mrs. White, I understand you have two little children at home. Who is taking care of them while you are here?"

"My mother."

"Then you will be able to concentrate on your duties here, and won't have to worry about picking up the kids by a certain time?"

"That's right."

"In fact, you wouldn't mind having a few days' vacation from your duties at home, would you?"

"That would be nice," she said, laughing.

CONCLUSION

Get involved in the kind of litigation with which you feel philosophically comfortable. Be a sincere kind of person! Let that sincerity shine through to the jury. Avoid at all expense even an appearance of what would compromise your credibility with the jury. Your client's lawsuit depends upon your establishing and maintaining credibility with the jury.

HOW DO YOU KNOW WHEN A CASE IS RIGHT FOR YOU?

1. Study your client at the first interview, be frank, don't be afraid of losing him or her as a client, warn the client as to the emotional challenge of litigation, and determine whether you and this client want to begin the long trek toward a jury verdict.
2. Study the kind of litigation in even further depth.
3. Consider carefully the extent to which the client may attempt to interfere with your trial strategy, your personal view of the client and lawsuit, and whether this is how you want to spend your career.
4. Consider whether the client can obtain other competent counsel if you do not accept the lawsuit.

JURORS BELIEVE WHEN THEY CAN IDENTIFY

The verdict in your lawsuit will depend upon the conclusion reached by people serving on the jury. Jurors reach conclusions on the basis of people and issues with which they can identify. Prepare and execute your lawsuit with this in mind.

Select Jurors Who Can Identify with Your Client
and His Cause

During *voir dire*, your questioning should be aimed at discovering ways in which prospective jurors can identify with your client and his or her cause. Understand why some people identify with certain other people.

People with similar backgrounds usually identify with each other. Immigrants of a country protested in large numbers when immigrants from the same country were convicted of a barroom gang rape. People who have been cheated by a large corporation will be sympathetic with a person who has been cheated by a large corporation, whereas, a person who has been mugged is not likely to have any sympathy for a person charged with robbery.

WARNING: Look for the exceptions! A black male executive may not want to identify with a black laborer. Women are not usually a woman's best friend in the courtroom.

Establish This Identity Throughout the Trial

Once you have jurors who can identify with your client and his or her cause, take advantage of it. Throughout the drama, let the audience enjoy this relationship it has with the characters of your drama. You don't have to hit them over the head with it, but let them know it is there!

Present your drama in terms that can be understood, in a way that is believable. This often can be accomplished with techniques of identity. People can identify with fear, hunger, embarrassment, and pain. Few people can identify with a wealthy person being "down to his last million" or with a pedophile who would prefer sex with a child rather than an adult.

EXAMPLE: GETTING THE JURY TO IDENTIFY
WITH YOUR CLIENT

A woman and her sister had spent the evening working at a beach hotel and stopped by a restaurant for a snack. As she passed a table, she noticed her husband holding hands with, and staring into the eyes of a beautiful young woman. She stopped and said, "Aren't you going to introduce me?" and "accidentally" knocked a kettle of hot water into the woman's lap.

"Accidentally"—now that is the key word to this potential courtroom drama. Try this word on your "unofficial jury panel" of friends and see if it sells. It did not!

People didn't believe the kettle of hot water ended up in the woman's lap by accident because they could identify with the client. They knew how they would feel if they found their husband with a beautiful young woman, and they knew that there is no way that kettle would end up in that lap accidentally. Ask them to sympathize with your client, but don't ask them to believe she didn't help that kettle topple over.

Fortunately, counsel took the deposition of the paramour turned victim, and fortunately she tried very hard to be a good witness—too hard, in fact. She testified that the water was "scalding hot," and that the woman had poured "the entire kettle" into her lap.

That called for a little investigation, so counsel went to the restaurant. While his wife poured the kettle of water into a large container, counsel clocked the process. Each time she did it, it took exactly nine seconds to pour the kettle of water.

You are now ready for trial, and ready to use something with which the jury could identify. What does nine seconds mean to you? It means a goal that was finally reached when a human being ran 100 yards in nine seconds flat. What does 100 yards mean to you? It means the distance of a football field. So, now you can stand before a jury and say, "Imagine a human being running from one end of a football field to another, and imagine that for that entire period of time a woman was just sitting there while scalding water was being poured into her lap." Jurors would be able to identify with what counsel was saying, because they have seen a human being run the distance of a football field, and they have jumped instantaneously from a shower when extremely hot water shot forth.

CONCLUSION

Select jurors who can identify, and then help them identify with your client by providing universal examples they can relate to. Once they identify with the situation, they'll believe your client, enhancing chances for a favorable verdict.

HOW TO DEVELOP UNIVERSAL EXAMPLES

1. Review the age, sex, employment, and other history of your client and your witnesses—determine how you can have them identify with jurors, such as a health problem of an older person.
2. Review the occurences that form your lawsuit, and see how jurors of common experience can identify, such as a client who forgot to fasten his or her seatbelt with a juror who admitted on *voir dire* that he or she has made the same mistake.

CHAPTER TEN

The Obligatory Scene
and Your Obligation
to the Jury

DELIVER WHAT YOU HAVE PROMISED

To win a verdict, you must arouse the jury's interest and sympathy, and satisfy that interest right in the middle of the courtroom.

EXAMPLE: *A MISSED OPPORTUNITY TO AROUSE SYMPATHY*

Plaintiff's attorney told the jury in opening statement that his client's mobile home had been burned to the ground. At that moment, the jurors pictured that fire and pictured what the home must have looked like after the fire. However, the plaintiff's attorney did not show a picture of the home as it looked after the fire. When plaintiff's attorney painted a picture for the jury that could have been portrayed fairly and accurately by a photo, he was obliged to present a photo, or a good explanation of why none was introduced.

Create Interest by Promising the Jury Something Is Going to Happen

What if you have a piece of paper that will simply blow the witness right out of his chair? Should you show this to him at deposition to pin him down, or wait and let the jury watch this dramatic moment of the trial? Remember, your chance of winning increases in proportion to the dramatic impact you can squeeze from this little piece of paper.

What you do will depend upon your strategy, and your strategy must have a goal. Your goal must be the settlement of a lawsuit as well as the winning of the lawsuit. If that evidence can get you as good a result out of court as you can get in court, you have a duty to your client to use it for this purpose.

If, however, the evidence will not obtain the desired settlement, you must then decide the moment at which it will have its most dramatic impact. Prepare the jury for that moment, without preparing opposing counsel:

"The prosecutor told you in his opening statement that he will bring John Brown into this courtroom as a witness for the State. Don't judge this man's testimony until you have heard all of it, the direct testimony and the cross-examination of this witness. Wait until you know all there is to be known during this trial about this witness, and then give his testimony whatever weight you think it might deserve, if any!"

The jury now knows you have something on this witness. They know you are going to show them what it is, and probably during cross-examination. You have now established the grounds for what playwrights call an obligatory scene, in which you are now obliged to show the jury, right in front of them, that there is good reason for them not to believe the witness.

When the judge announces, "You may examine the witness," the eyes of the jury will turn to you as though to say it is time for you to produce. Lay the groundwork carefully. The jury does not object to a mounting of interest and suspense. Have the exhibit properly marked and inspected by opposing counsel. Let the jury stare at the paper as you hold it where they can see it. Ask a few questions to set the stage.

"You have sworn to tell this jury the truth, have you not?"
"Yes."
"And you just told the jury that you remembered being with my client on the night he is charged with robbing the store?"
"Yes."
"Do you recognize the paper I just handed you?"
"Yes. It is a letter I wrote from . . ."
"From where, Mr. Brown?"
"From Philadelphia."
"And what is the date of that letter?"
"January 17, 1981."
"Isn't that the date you told this jury you were with my client at the Rose Tavern?"
"Yes."

"Mr. Brown, please read the first paragraph of that letter to the jury."

"Dear Bill, I have been in Philadelphia with my aunt for a few weeks, but expect to come back next week. I will call you so we can get together."

You have kept your promise to the jury!

Make It Happen in the Courtroom—with Drama

Get your witnesses, including experts, into the courtroom, if at all possible. In your opening statement, you have told the jury that the greatest brain surgeon in the world is going to walk into that courtroom and testify for your client. They are anxious to see this famous person, and when he appears in the form of a written deposition they will be disappointed. Don't imply a promise you cannot fulfill.

EXAMPLE: SHOWING THE JURY WHAT YOU'VE PROMISED

Counsel hinted during voir dire, and promised during opening statement, that he would show the jury that this large corporation took advantage of his client when they had her sign the contract. He envisioned a scene in which he would accomplish this and "promised" it, but as the trial progressed the scene just did not develop as he had hoped.

Then as opposing counsel began his final argument, counsel noticed he was holding the contract in his hand and soon was telling the jury to take that document with them to the jury room and study it during its deliberation. Counsel remembered that during trial, for some unknown reason, opposing counsel doodled on the contract.

Feeling he had nothing to lose, counsel jumped to his feet and said, "Your Honor, I object to the jury examining this exhibit because opposing counsel has marked on the exhibit, he has changed the exhibit, and he did so after the exhibit was admitted into evidence by this court." Opposing counsel was surprised and embarrassed.

He started blurting, "I didn't do anything wrong. I just wrote on the side of the document." Counsel graciously agreed that the jury could examine the document, if opposing counsel would show the jury what writing was his and what was already written on the document. Opposing counsel agreed and spent most of his final argument explaining this to the jury.

When counsel rose to give his final argument, he made it very clear to the jury that he was not suggesting that opposing counsel had done anything wrong. He held the contract in his left hand and a pen in his right hand. He then said, "However, as long as opposing counsel sees nothing wrong with writing on an exhibit, I am going to underline the one sentence in this contract I want you to remember."

He underscored that sentence twice, while opposing counsel was jumping to his feet shouting, "I object, your Honor," then he turned to counsel and said, "You can't do that!" Counsel calmly replied, "But I just did." Opposing counsel stood there for a moment, trying to figure out what to do next, then everyone in the courtroom broke into laughter.

WARNING: Don't ever embarrass another human being in front of the jury unless you are positive the jury wants that person to be embarrassed, and that is not very often. Counsel was getting dangerously close to making a big mistake, so he let the jury and opposing counsel know it was in good fun.

"I want you to know that I have known this lawyer for many years and I may joke with him, but I will never question his integrity. I can't say the same for this big corporation he represents, however, and to be very serious with you, that is why I wanted to underline that one sentence in the contract.

"That one sentence tells you all you want to know about this corporation. It is just one sentence, and it is in small print, and it is tucked away in the middle of the contract, but it tells you this corporation took advantage of this lady.

"Opposing counsel told you this is an iron-clad contract. It had better be an iron-clad contract, this corporation paid some big law firm in Chicago a lot of money to draft it, and paid some printer a few dollars to hide this sentence in small print in the middle of the page.

"But let me tell you something about an iron-clad contract, it can be the most perfect contract ever written and it is absolutely worthless if it is fraudulently obtained. The letters on this contract could be printed in gold, but this woman's signature on that contract doesn't mean a thing if she didn't willingly and knowingly sign this piece of paper. You will remember when I cross-examined their witness, this man representing this corporation who signed the contract on behalf of the corporation, did not know this sentence was in the contract, so how could my client be expected to know?"

The jury was out long enough to (a) select a foreman, and (b) read one sentence of the contract. They then returned a verdict for the woman and I am sure that verdict was at least partly based on a scene that dramatically showed the jurors what counsel had promised he would show them.

CONCLUSION

Don't hesitate to make a firm promise to the jury as to what you are going to prove. However, make sure you can keep the promise. Look for ways of keeping the promise by using courtroom drama.

WAYS TO KEEP YOUR PROMISES TO THE JURY

1. Determine what you must prove.
2. Determine what additional proof will help your cause.
3. Prepare your case to assure that proof.
4. Promise what you know you can prove.
5. Qualify your promise where there is any likelihood your proof may fall short of your promise.

USE SHOW AND TELL TIME

Playwrights have used demonstrative evidence for centuries. Its use in the American courtroom is expanding as trial lawyers show the jury as much of the story as they can.

Determine What Proof Can Be Accomplished with Physical Evidence

When you prepare your trial notebook, cram everything into that notebook except that which follows the divider marked "EVIDENCE." There you will list exhibits that are far too large to fit into any notebook.

A layperson can see broken bones in an X-ray. The jurors can understand why a device failed to function if they see it live in the courtroom. The jurors can picture the scene of an accident if they see a large photo of the scene.

Don't explain it if you can show it. When you do show it, do not let the explaining precede or override the showing in a way that will detract from it. Use your witnesses to call attention to or explain the exhibit, but let the exhibit be stage center!

EXAMPLE: EXHIBITING PHYSICAL EVIDENCE WITH DRAMA

"Mrs. Smith, did this big corporation tell you they would refund the money?"

"Yes."

(*Stop!* Don't let her explain what you want the exhibit to demonstrate.)

"Mrs. Smith, I show you what has been marked plaintiff's exhibit 13. Do you recognize it?"

"Yes. It is a letter I received from the company."

"When did you receive it?"

"After my conference with the manager."

"At that conference, did the manager tell you that you would get the refund?"

"He said I would have gotten it if I had notified the company within a year."

"Mrs. Smith, would you read this letter from the company to the jury?"

"Why, of course. 'Dear Mrs. Smith: This is to acknowledge receipt of notice within a year of your purchase . . .'"

Determine When and How You Can Use Demonstrative Evidence

Plan what you can show the jury and when you should show it. Space the introduction of exhibits. Use exhibits when the jury's attention is high. Alert the jury to the fact that this is a very special time in the telling of your story.

EXAMPLE: INTRODUCING EXHIBITS AT THE RIGHT TIME

"Mrs. Wilson, do you know, of your own knowledge, that John Banes knew this woman?"

"Yes, I am positive."

"You know that he came into this courtroom and testified under oath that he had never met her?"

"I heard him, but he is not telling the truth."

"How do you know this?"

"I have a photograph of them."

"Is this a group picture, one in which he may not have known he was being photographed with her?"

"No, Counselor. It is a photograph of just the two of them, and you can tell from it that they definitely know each other."

"Do you happen to have that photograph with you?"

"Yes, I have it here in my purse."

Marking photos in advance saves time and lessens interruptions to your presentation. However, there are times when you want to drain each moment of drama from the scene. The jurors look at the purse, watch her take the photo from it, watch the attorney walk to the reporter to have it marked as an exhibit, watch the attorney show it to opposing counsel, and even try to read opposing counsel's mind. That little photograph should receive all of this attention!

Use Exhibits with Drama

Don't let the jury get tired of an exhibit, before or after its introduction. Treat the exhibit as something special, and the jury will consider it as something special.

Use Experiments—with Caution

Conduct experiments in the courtroom when you are positive they will work. There is nothing that will prove your case more convincingly than conducting an experiment that works right in front of the jury's eyes. There is nothing that will lose the case quicker than having the experiment explode in your face.

EXAMPLE: CONDUCTING AN EXPERIMENT TO ADD TO THE DRAMA

An attorney was planning a courtroom demonstration that would prove the fire could not have started from the source charged by opposing counsel. The attorney decided to test the experiment, prior to the trial. He recreated the same condition in a vacant building to prove that a fire could not result from such a condition. Flames burst into the air, and a quick response from the fire department saved the building, but not the lawsuit.

Consider conducting the experiment in front of your video camera. You can then run the tape and see how the experiment works. If it is a success you can try to get the video admitted, with an explanation by an expert, and not have a live performance in the courtroom. The judge may be happy to avoid the danger of courtroom experiments, and counsel will know in advance that he or she is not going to burn the courthouse to the ground.

EXAMPLE: PRESENTING VISUAL EVIDENCE

The news media had "convicted" a young man of attempting to run over and kill a police officer. In addition to the felony charge, there were several charges of municipal violations.

Counsel arrived at city hall with his court reporter and cross-examined the officer at length about where he was and where the young man's car was at various times. From the transcript of this cross-examination, counsel drafted a diagram to use before the jury in the felony case.

The diagram, shown in Figure 10-1, shows where the officer, A, was, and where the car, B, was when the officer first saw the car (see line 1). Then when the car was only fifty yards away, the officer is shown as C and the car as D (see line 2). Immediately before the officer jumped, he was E and the car was F. It is obvious from this diagram that the car was not moving toward the officer, as he claimed, but, in fact, the officer was moving toward the middle of the road in front of the car. This was something the jury could easily understand.

The officer had told the chief, and the news media, that the young man had tried to run him down. The truth was that at no time did the young man move his car from the middle of the road. On the other hand, the officer admitted he was moving toward the middle of the road and jumped when the car did not stop.

Cross-examination made clear with "show and tell" kept this young man from jail.

CONCLUSION

The jury can see more clearly when visual evidence is presented.

HOW TO USE VISUAL EVIDENCE MOST EFFECTIVELY

1. Determine what can be presented more dramatically with visual evidence.
2. Explain visual evidence *before* the jury sees it.
3. Let the jury know *why* this proof is being presented with visual evidence.
4. Choose the right moment to present visual evidence and determine how long the visual evidence should remain before the jury.

Figure 10-1   Show and Tell Time

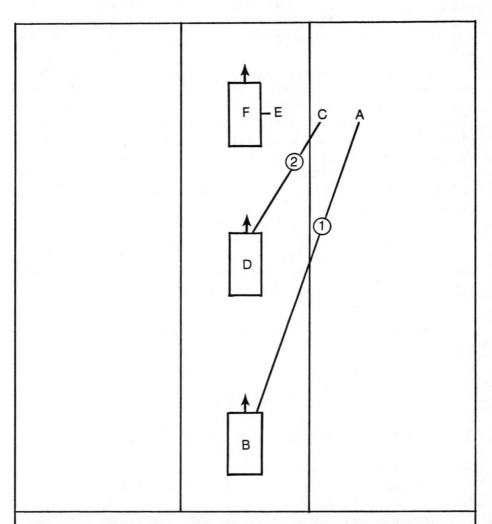

The officer claimed the car tried to run into him. His testimony, however, was that when the car was first seen by him he was at *A*, and the car at *B*, a distance of 100 yards (line 1) away. When the car was 50 yards away (line 2) he was at *C* and the car was at *D*. Immediately before he jumped to avoid the car, he was at *E* and the car at *F*. From this diagram, the jury could conclude the car did not run down the officer; the officer was, in fact, moving toward the path of the car.

KEEP PROMISES AND BUILD CREDIBILITY

Building credibility is what the trial of a lawsuit is all about. You can build credibility by keeping big and little promises.

Don't Build Up Expectations
That Might Not Be Fulfilled

Winning your case early means promising the jury proof. Don't, however, overpromise as to the amount of proof, or as to the form of proof. If you expect to use a deposition in place of a live witness, prepare the jury for this. If the doctor is out of the operating room earlier than expected . . . surprise, we have him here in person.

When Expectations Are Not Fulfilled,
Let the Jury Know Why

If you feel safe in promising the presence of an eye witness and an emergency arises, explain that situation in front of the jury!

"Mr. Wright, you may call your next witness."
"Your Honor, my next witness was to be John Smith, but he was hit by a truck on the way to court and is now in the hospital."

Protect your credibility with the jury at all expense. Your client's lawsuit may depend upon it.

Tie in the Fulfillment of Expectations
with Your Credibility

Be subtle about it, but make sure the jury knows you have kept your promises. Reaffirm your professionalism in a professional way.

EXAMPLES: *You have boasted during opening statement that you will put a special expert on the stand, then get all of his/or her credentials into evidence, and let the jury see that you have produced. You promised you would produce an eye witness and you*

did, remind the jury about it during final argument. You warned
that the defendant could not be believed, and you devastated him or
her on cross-examination again, remind the jury of this during final
argument.

EXAMPLE: PLACING EMPHASIS ON THE
FINAL ARGUMENT

There is one obligatory scene in every courtroom drama, and that is
the final argument. Jurors have seen movies and television shows
and know that this is the most dramatic moment in the trial. If you
don't place importance on final argument, you will lose credibility
with the jury.

> "Where was John Hawkins when his mother was in
> the hospital? Where was he during those entire thirty-one
> days? He was busy. He told you he was so busy he did not
> have time to drive fifty miles to visit his mother. Not once
> during those thirty-one days.
> "Where was John Hawkins last Christmas, when his
> mother was home recuperating from those thirty-one days
> in the hospital? Oh, he remembered his mother, he sent her
> a card from Hawaii. Not a present, just a card from Hawaii.
> "And where was John Hawkins yesterday morning?
> You and I know where he was yesterday morning, he was
> right here in this courtroom trying to get as much money as
> he can from his mother's estate. (After a pause) It is too late
> for John Hawkins to visit his mother in the hospital. It is
> too late for him to be with his mother during this Christmas
> or any Christmas. But, you know something else? It is too
> late for him to get any money from his mother or from his
> mother's estate."

The cross-examination of John Hawkins was a lawyer's dream,
but it was merely the laying of groundwork for final argument.

The jurors heard the cross-examination of John Hawkins, but
they needed to hear about it again during final argument to
strengthen their thoughts that this man did not deserve his mother's

money. It was important for them to watch him sit there squirming and listen to the truth, his eyes downcast, his shoulders slumped.

CONCLUSION

If you feel that jurors want or expect a certain thing to happen, make it happen. Expecting the action to come from you is to your advantage, but not delivering what the jurors expect breaches that faith in a way that is devastating to your client.

HOW TO ALWAYS DELIVER THE ACTION

1. Don't even hint that such action will occur until you know you can make it happen.
2. Prepare your direct evidence so you will know exactly what will happen and when it will happen.
3. Through effective discovery know what you can show on cross-examination.
4. Try your lawsuit with a thoroughness that enables you to deliver your final argument with the action possible after showing the law and evidence to be on your side.

CHAPTER ELEVEN

Recesses

THE JURY NEVER RESTS—NOR DOES
THE TRIAL LAWYER WHO WANTS TO WIN

The jury has a limited attention span and it is necessary to have recesses. This is very important in the courtroom drama, where it takes time to tell a story. The trial lawyer needs to capture that "I-couldn't-put-the-book-down" fascination.

Plan Your Recesses as a Part
of Your Courtroom Drama

The trial lawyer asked his witness several questions that had little to do with what he was trying to prove. Finally, he got to his story and the jury began to listen. Just as the testimony was about to reveal the most important part of the story, the judge said, "I think it is time to recess until tomorrow morning."

This can be avoided! Know how long it will take to tell the dramatic part of the story and fit it into a segment of the trial you know will not be interrupted.

Recesses are important. How much time should you plan between recesses? How should the segments between recesses be structured? What should happen right before a recess? Answering these questions will help plan your courtroom drama.

Participate in the Judge's Decisions Relating to Recess

There are literally thousands of appellate decisions telling the trial lawyer that the trial judge has broad discretionary powers relative to the conduct of a trial. Not one of those decisions, however, prevents the lawyer from saying, "Your Honor, I wonder if we could take our recess just a little early so I won't be interrupted in the middle of my cross-examination?" Even if you can't budge the judge one minute from his schedule, you should try to learn the schedule the judge is going to follow, so you can adjust accordingly.

You and Every Character of Your Drama Are on Display During Recess

Cases have been lost by what the jurors observed during recess. The plaintiff who is so serious while in session gives a different impression if laughing and joking during recess. The client who claims difficulty in walking and walks briskly during recess causes jurors to wonder. Your credibility is being tested during recess.

You and every member of your cast are on display during recess. It usually is best if not one person in your courtroom drama be anywhere near the jury during recess. All of your trial participants should use the restrooms on a different floor and eat lunch at a different restaurant.

ALTERNATE STRATEGY: I know there are those who purposely "display" their cast during recess, and if they are successful, I cannot argue with that. However, I find "displaying" the cast properly during trial is enough of a task. I also know that some courthouses have but one restaurant nearby, and lawyers who practice in such communities feel comfortable with the folksiness of judge, jury, witnesses, and attorneys breaking bread within close range. It requires some effort on the part of the trial lawyer not to lose ground and to avoid the temptation to gain ground improperly during recess.

You can present your drama as professionally as possible, and then during a recess destroy all the work you have done. If a dramatic actor intermingled with the audience during intermission, smiling and laughing at the audience, he may find it difficult to change the atmosphere instantaneously and to regain the earlier impression.

The audience at a courtroom drama demands that the drama be genuine. A doctor who describes a serious injury projects an image that may be shattered, as he laughs and jokes about his golf score in the corridor moments later. A person may suspect that his doctor plays golf—just as a child may suspect that his parents make love—but when a person is lying on an operating table he feels comfortable with the doctor image that is manifesting confidence.

Figure 11-1   One Trial Judge's Schedule

```
 8:00   Lawyers should be meeting with clients and witnesses

 9:00   Lawyers should be available to the court

 9:30   Jurors should be in jury box and lawyers seated at the
        counsel table

10:30   Recess

10:45   Return from recess

12:00   Recess for lunch

 1:30   Return from lunch

 3:30   Recess

 3:45   Return from recess

 5:00   Adjourn for day

 5:00   Lawyers should be available to court

 5:30   Lawyers should meet with client or witnesses

 7:30   Lawyers should prepare for the following day of trial

        NOTE:   (1) Every trial judge has a different schedule

                (2) Some judges are very flexible, others
                    walk off the bench at a certain hour and
                    refuse requests to vary schedule
```

Figure 11-2   Typical Time Requirements (Three-day Jury Trial)

		Hours
1. *Voir Dire*		3.0
2. Plaintiff's opening statement		0.5
3. Defendant's opening statement		0.5
4. Plaintiff's case:		
a. Witness Jones	2.0	
b. Witness Smith	0.5	
c. Witness Brown	1.0	
d. Witness White	0.7	
e. Witness Blue	0.3	
f. Witness Doe	1.5	
g. Passing Exhibits	0.5	
h. Reading Defendant's Deposition	0.25	
Total		6.5
5. Defendant's case		8.00
6. Rebuttal		1.00
7. Plaintiff's final argument		0.5
8. Defendant's final argument		0.5
9. Instructions to jury		0.25

Note: This is just an *estimate*. This is a *picture* the trial lawyer must keep in his mind. By keeping this general time framework in mind, he can better organize his courtroom drama.

Courtroom drama is a series of images, so you must avoid doing anything that is going to destroy an image that is favorable to your cause. If there is a danger of overexposing a member of your cast in the courtroom, you certainly do not want to extend that exposure into the recess.

Parents should avoid bringing children to the courtroom. Children do not react well to a courtroom environment, and during intermission jurors will watch the nice lady who has just testified become stern, or worse, fail to control the child the way the juror would.

Schedule Your Recesses

Visualize the judge's schedule. If necessary, write it down, as I have in Figure 11-1. Plan your trial, and assign estimated time requirements for each part of your trial, especially the direct testimony. (See Figure 11-2.) Eventually, you will do all of this in your head, but you will do it, if you want to be able to plan your trial and your recesses.

If the judge said, "You may call your next witness," and it is thirty minutes before lunch, you must look at your time requirement notes and make a decision. Call a fifteen-minute witness, if it does not interfere with the structuring of your drama.

You will consider many factors, in addition to the time requirement factor. You want to include among those factors, the need to start with a good witness, and to use certain witnesses at a stage of a trial when they will have the most dramatic impact. Use a time schedule, but don't be a slave to it!

You may want to use that time something like this:

"Your Honor, I want to call Ellen Jones, my client, as my first witness, but I would first like to read into evidence the defendant's deposition."

"You may do so."

"Your Honor, I am reading from page 13, line 3.

"Question: By whom are you employed?"

"Able Construction Company."

"Were you so employed on June 1, 1982?"

"Yes."

"In what capacity?"

"As a truck driver."

"What were you doing at 3:15 P.M. on that date?"

"Delivering some food. I had just picked up the food at the wholesaler's warehouse."

"Did the truck you were driving collide with an automobile at that time?"

"Yes."

"Will you tell me how that happened?"

"Yes."

"Please do."

"I was driving my truck east on Watson and was following the car driven by this lady. I did not notice that the light had changed and she had come to a stop, and I drove into the back of her car."

You are keeping within the timeframe, yet you are telling our story. You are doing it with evidence that will convince the jury. You are off to a good start, and the judge who insisted that you not break for lunch before starting the trial may feel the reading of the deposition was enough to get us into the case, and not insist that you proceed with live testimony before lunch.

EXAMPLE: USING RECESSES TO YOUR ADVANTAGE

The State had listed six eye witnesses it would call to testify in a murder trial. Counsel prepared six copies of the diagram of the scene of the alleged murder.

During cross-examination of the first eye witness, counsel had him mark the exhibit to show where the victim was, where the defendant was, and where the eye witnesses were at the time of the stabbing. When he began his cross-examination of the second eye witness, he used the second copy of the same diagram.

The prosecutor objected and the judge called the attorneys to the sidebar. The prosecutor insisted that counsel should use the same exhibit he had used while cross-examining the first witness. Counsel told the judge if the State feared two eye witnesses would mark the exhibits differently, thus giving conflicting testimony, then the court had no duty to protect witnesses who may give conflicting testimony, especially in a murder trial. The judge agreed.

The second witness did make a few variations, not enough to hang him, but if this trend continued, counsel may have had six witnesses with six different views of where people were at the time of the stabbing. However, a funny thing happened on the way to acquittal.

The judge recessed for the day at the end of the testimony of the second witness, and the following morning it was a new ballgame. Every one of the remaining four witnesses marked their exhibits exactly the same. Such recesses can destroy your case.

This technique can be used in a personal injury case, where there are several eye witnesses. Perhaps you can find a case in which all eye witnesses will testify without a recess during which they can prepare for the remaining testimony.

Use Recesses to Regroup

Regrouping is a two-edged sword! Use it when you need to, just as it will be used against you. When a woman seems confused and is about to make some blunders, look for the slightest tear that might enable you to say, "Your Honor, it is obvious that Mrs. Jones has been very upset over this entire incident. I wonder if we can have a five-minute recess so she can pull herself together."

You have forced opposing counsel to object to what is a humane request. You have forced the judge to permit the recess, or have the jury question his wisdom for the first time during the trial. You have avoided telling the jury that you are concerned that the witness may say something you do not want the witness to say.

If the judge rules against you, pray that the tears increase to the point where the judge has no choice. There is a thin, gray line in such a situation. The more emotional a witness becomes, the more apt she is to make blunders, and the more apt the judge is to grant a brief recess. As the need increases, the risk increases, and the responsibility of the trial lawyer increases. No lawyer lost brownie points showing concern for a witness.

CONCLUSION

Plan every aspect of your trial with recesses in mind. Try to have the recesses occur when you want them to occur, but when this is not possible, work around recesses, hold up on certain testimony, even stall when necessary (without making it obvious to the judge you are stalling) but don't let recesses adversely affect your courtroom drama.

HOW TO USE RECESSES TO YOUR ADVANTAGE

1. Time recesses to end a part of the trial immediately before a recess.
2. Adjust the speed of the trial to give you an opportunity to talk with a witness during recess.
3. Time recesses so what jurors think about during recess is positive toward your client and his or her cause.
4. Use the last few minutes prior to recess to build the juror's interest and expectation for the next part of your courtroom presentation.

LEAVE THEM ANXIOUS FOR THE NEXT SCENE OF THE DRAMA

The most important part of recess planning is planning that final moment before the trial adjourns for recess. The trial lawyer must prepare for that moment with expertise.

One playwright said he never lets the curtain come down at the end of a scene unless he is positive the audience wants that curtain to go up again. That is excellent advice for a trial lawyer. Too often, we send a jury out for lunch completely indifferent as to whether they ever return to the courtroom.

Pique their interest! Tell the story in well-planned segments. End the scene as though you are ending a chapter, not a book with suspense. End the segment as though you are saying, "Hurry back and hear the rest."

End the Scene with Drama

Jurors are not supposed to discuss the case with anyone during recess, but they have been known to do so. A juror is not prohibited from thinking about the case during recess and this he or she will always do. Consider the recency rule! The juror will be thinking about what he has just seen or heard, so make sure what he or she is thinking about is what might help you win your lawsuit.

That last moment before recess must not only tell a good message, it must do it with drama. Let the jury know you are concluding a segment of your trial. Say it with words and with impact. Let the jury know that when they come back they will be in for a treat.

Let the Jury Know That the Very Next Part of the Trial Is Important

"Your Honor, opposing counsel and I have agreed that we will take Doctor Smith out of turn and put him on the stand right after lunch, so he can get to Harvard University in time to deliver his lecture to the thirty leading brain specialists who have flown in from around the world to hear what Dr. Smith has to say on this subject."

You must also let the jury know that the closing moments of this session are important. You can do this by making them important. You can tell them what is coming after recess, by building up to what is to come after recess.

"Mr. Jones, you have testified that there was a knife?"
"Yes."
"Did you see the knife?"
"Yes."
"Was anyone else present when you saw the defendant with the knife?"
"Yes. Albert Smith."
"Now, Mr. Smith is going to testify right after lunch, so I would like for you to tell the jury where Mr. Smith was standing at the time you saw the defendant with the knife."
"He was standing right next to the defendant."
"Did you hear the defendant say something to Mr. Smith?"
"I heard him say something, but I wasn't close enough to understand what he was saying."
"How close was Mr. Smith to the defendant when the defendant made these statements?"
"Just a few feet."

"I show you what has been marked Exhibit 3. What is it?"

"It is the knife I have been talking about."

"Your Honor, I would like to introduce Plaintiff's Exhibit 3 into evidence."

"Any objection?"

"No, Your Honor."

"It is admitted."

"I have no further questions, but I would like to pass the exhibit among the jurors."

"You may."

You have ended the morning session with the jury examining an important piece of evidence. You have prompted the jury to think about the conversation between the defendant and the next witness. The members of the jury know that they will find out about that conversation when they return from lunch.

You can keep the jury interested by keeping them informed as to your schedule:

1. Let them know what has been done.

   "Doctor, you have explained how this injury will affect my client's chances of returning to his former employment. Will you now tell the jury . . ."

2. Let them know the purpose of the present testimony.

   "What did you find when you inspected the bolt?"
   "I found it was broken."
   "In your opinion, Mr. Brown, could that have caused the accident?"
   "Oh, yes, that is definitely what caused the accident."

3. Let them know what evidence is going to follow:

   "I understand, Mr. Jones, that after lunch you will show a video tape?"
   "Yes."

"What will be the purpose of the tape?"

"The tape will show the condition of the property before and after the damage done by the defendant."

EXAMPLE: STRUCTURING EACH TRIAL SEGMENT TO END WITH IMPACT

Trial lawyers want short cross-examinations in one piece, and long cross-examinations in intelligent segments. What do you do, however, when the judge insists upon your using the last half hour of the day to begin your cross-examination? Let the jury know the real cross-examination is to take place the following morning, and use that half hour to whet their appetite.

"Your Honor, I need a lot more than half an hour to cross-examine this witness, but I think I can get some of the preliminaries out of the way this afternoon. Mr. Jones, you testified that my client had written you about this matter, is that right?"

"Yes."

"When was that?"

"Last summer."

"Was that in the form of a letter?"

"Yes."

"Is there some reason you destroyed the letter?"

"I did not destroy the letter."

"Do you have it in court with you?"

"No one asked me to bring it."

"Now, Mr. Jones, you knew you were going to testify here today, did you not?"

"Yes."

"Is there some reason you did not bring the letter, so this jury could see it, if you were going to testify about it?"

Opposing counsel rises to object.

"Your Honor, I withdraw that question. Let me ask you this, Mrs. Jones, where is that letter at this very moment?"

"At home."

"Then you can bring that letter to court with you
tomorrow morning?"

"Yes. I guess so."

"Would you be kind enough to do that?"

"Yes."

"Now, you wrote my client a letter soon after that, did
you not?"

"Yes."

The attorney walked back to the counsel table and picked up a
letter. "Your Honor, I would like to have this marked as Plaintiff's
Exhibit No. 15." The exhibit was marked and counsel handed it to
opposing counsel to inspect. The jury was very interested in the
piece of paper. They also were interested in the piece of paper that
the witness was to bring to court the following morning.

"Mr. Jones you wrote this letter on August 15, did you not?"

"Yes, that is the date."

"I want to ask you some questions about this letter, and the
letter you are to bring to court in the morning, but first, I have a few
questions about your testimony as it relates to another matter." The
scene was set. The interest of the jury was aroused. They knew the
remaining twenty minutes of this afternoon's cross-examination
would not amount to much, but they were interested in returning the
following morning.

A recess can be very helpful. All the discovery afforded you by
the modern rules of procedure do not prepare you for every
eventuality. All the briefing a witness can receive may not fully
prepare that witness for the real live courtroom.

After the cross-examination of a witness, the judge called a
recess, and counsel said to the witness:

"You didn't tell me about the check to Mr. Jones."

"I forgot."

"When the lawyer asked you about it you seemed very
uncertain as though you were hiding something."

"I was embarrassed that I had not told you, and had
forgotten to tell about it on my deposition."

"Was there some reason to forget?"

"I think it was because it was for such a small amount,
and I didn't expect him to pay it back."

"Do you have the cancelled check?"

"Sure."

"Bring it to court tomorrow morning, and I will use it
on re-direct."

Counsel had time to talk with his client. His client had time to obtain an exhibit. Counsel could then rehabilitate the client as a witness.

All of this because of a recess.

CONCLUSION

Structure each "scene" so it ends with a bang, and with an invitation for your audience to return. Let the jury know what is going to happen when they return. You can do this as a natural part of the dialogue. If all else fails, just tell them (usually through remarks to the judge) what is going to happen.

NOTES ON WHICH TO END A SCENE

1. "Your witness" tells the jury that you have finished off this witness.
2. "After lunch I will call my eye witness, your Honor" tells the jurors to hurry back from lunch and watch the excitement.
3. "Mrs. Smith, during the lunch hour, will you get the cancelled check and bring it to court so the jury can see it?" tells the jury that you are about to substantiate something.
4. "That is plaintiff's case, Your Honor" tells the jury. END OF CHAPTER.

CHAPTER TWELVE

Conflict:
The Essence
of Drama

CONTROL CONFLICT, OR IT WILL CONTROL YOU

Conflict is the heart of courtroom drama. The trial lawyer must appreciate the importance of the influence of conflict in his courtroom drama, or he will be unable to control it.

We love conflict, but we want it to be good conflict. We feel sorry for a team that is losing by 100 points, and we feel sorry for a little old lady who is confused as a lawyer cross-examines her. We want conflict to be fair, above all else.

If there is no conflict, there is no lawsuit. You are in court because there is a conflict. Make conflict an "old friend," with whom you will spend your life as a trial lawyer.

EXAMPLE: RECOGNIZING THE NATURE OF CONFLICT

"There were two eye witnesses to this accident, and they will tell you two different stories. You will have to listen to these two witnesses and decide what actually happened.

"John Jones, an off-duty police officer, will tell you he saw this young man drive through the red light and collide with my client. An elderly gentleman will tell you a different story, and I am sure this gentleman will tell you his story as he remembers it.

"Our evidence will show, however, that this gentleman was standing 200 feet from the collision, that his view was partially blocked, and that he is not positive what happened. Listen carefully to both of these witnesses, but don't form an opinion until you hear all of the evidence."

Counsel has:

1. *Let the jury know there will be conflict, so there is a reason for them to listen to the evidence carefully;*
2. *Told the jury there will be two different versions and has been fair in implying the jury should choose his version because of valid reasons such as distance from accident and obstruction of view, and not because one witness is elderly and the other is an off-duty police officer; and*
3. *Treated conflict as an old friend, not fearing it, but welcoming it with confidence he will win the conflict.*

Beginning lawyers fear conflict, and this fear causes them to settle cases that should be tried. Learn to use conflict and it will help you win.

How to Use Conflict with Drama

Here are some tips that will help you prepare your conflict with drama.

If a photo will help you win a major conflict, plaster that photo on your office wall and look at it every day, from the day the photo is taken until the day it is introduced into evidence.

EXAMPLE: BECOMING VERY FAMILIAR WITH AN EXHIBIT

The doctor had left a clamp in a woman's body following surgery, and the positive of the X-ray sat next to counsel's desk for more than a year. He listened to the reaction of people as they looked at that photo and catalogued them in his mind.

He also thought about that case more often than if it were tucked away in an exhibit drawer. By trial, counsel had memorized the exact location of that clamp at the time of the second operation, and from where it had migrated.

This exhibit was the center of conflict, and counsel became very familiar with the role this exhibit could play in resolving conflicts that would arise at trial.

If one sentence in a deposition will help you win a major conflict, memorize it, and wrap it in different sentences until it forms the focus of a paragraph that is going to be dynamite at the trial.

EXAMPLE: MEMORIZING A SENTENCE FROM A DEPOSITION

During final argument, counsel told the jury:

"Let me read to you what the defendant admitted was his testimony at the deposition: 'I hit the boy, but I had a right to.' We now know he did not have a right to. When he hit that boy he violated the law, but he did worse than that, he placed himself above the law, and that is something we cannot let people do in America."

From the moment the defendant's words were spoken at the deposition, counsel knew he would use that sentence during final argument. When he received the copy of the deposition, he photocopied it, enlarged it, and memorized it. By closing argument, he knew how to use it.

When you understand conflict you can appreciate the means of controlling it. Of all means available to you, none is more important than the conflict of cross-examination. This conflict is at its most sophisticated and fascinating height, when a good trial attorney cross-examines a witness.

Organize Conflict for Cross-Examination

A trial lawyer must focus in on conflict. Here is a practice that helps me "focus in." This practice can best be demonstrated by studying my legal pad, as shown in Figure 12-1.

Let us begin the cross-examination reflected in those notes. As opposing counsel is examining his witness, make entries in the right column. I already know what the answers are, because of the depositions. However, whether they are covered on direct or not, I want to cover them on cross, because I want the jury to hear them, from the defendant's own mouth.

Figure 12-1   Legal Pad Used for Cross-Examination

CROSS OF D	
TESTIMONY	QUETIONS

1 AGE –68
2 GOING TO WORK
3 ACC: 7:15 PM
4 DUE/WORK 7:30 PM
5 ACC: 4th/MAIN
6 WORK – McD
10th/CAROLINA
 	
THE ABOVE MEANS:
 	
(this column is for reference only)
 	
1. Witness is 68 years old.
2. Witness was going to work.
3. Accident occurred at 7:15 P.M.
4. Witness was due at work at 7:30 P.M.
5. Accident occurred at 4th and Main.
6. Witness works at McDonnell; at 10th and Carolina.
	1. DIST. D SAW IT
	   DEPO 12-8 150'
	2. D TOLD officer
	   "DID NOT SEE IT"
	   DEPO 14-6
	3. D TOLD IT
	   "HAD TWO DRINKS"
	4. HOW LONG
	   PKC/WORK (30 MIN)
	
	(this column is for areas you will question)
	
	1. What is distance witness was from scene? (on page 12, line 8 of her depo she said 150 feet)
	2. What did she tell officer? (in her depo she said, "Did not see it" page 14, line 6)
	3. What did defendant tell Plaintiff? In depo (page 17, line 3 he said "Had 2 drinks)
	4. How long would it take to get from scene of accident to work? (about 30 minutes)

"How old are you?"

"Sixty-eight."

"Where were you going?"

"To work."

"What time did the accident happen?"

"At 7:15 P.M."

"When were you due at work?"

"At 7:30 P.M."

"Where did this accident happen?"

"At Fourth and Main."

"Where do you work?"

"McDonnells, at Tenth and Carolina."

By now, I have made entries 1 through 6 under "Testimony." I now write four questions under "Questions," so I will be able to find the testimony quickly, though much of this may not be used in my cross-examination.

I may want to know that her age is sixty-eight, but probably not during cross-examination and probably not during final argument. However, if opposing counsel argues that his client could see perfectly because nothing was blocking her view, I might want, during rebuttal, to suggest that a 68-year-old woman who was not wearing glasses may not be able to see perfectly.

That's the kind of information I enter in the left column of a legal pad. Most of it will never need to be retrieved, but if it is needed, it is there.

The right column contains a list of questions that I will ask, or more accurately, the line of questioning I will pursue. This is a list of conflicts I can win. If I cannot win the conflict, or at least lessen the damage caused on direct, I don't want to talk about it. I don't want to give the witness an opportunity to repeat anything damaging to my cause.

As the direct examination continues, the list of testimonies and the list of questions grows. However, the list of "Questions" would grow. However, the list of "questions" should be very limited. By the time opposing counsel says, "Your witness," you have from two to ten subjects of questioning you want to pursue. Some experts say not more than three, but others say this is governed by the complexity of the lawsuit, and the testimony of the witness on direct.

USE CONFLICT TO KEEP THE JURY'S ATTENTION

Conflict catches the jury's attention, and if developed properly will keep the jury's attention. Conflict should be structured and prepared dramatically. Some sports announcers can make the dullest game exciting, and others can make the most exciting game sound dull. Harry Carey never says, "It's a home run." He says, "It might be, it could be, it *is* a home run!"

USE CONFLICT TO BRING JURORS TO YOUR SIDE

What people like most about conflict is that they can identify with one side. It is they who are punching the bad guy in the barroom brawl, sliding into second with a double, or being cheated by some huge corporation. Find a good conflict in your lawsuit, one you can get on the good side of, and establish jury-identity with it during the *voir-dire.*
     This can be accomplished, if you will:

1. Make a list of issues that will arise during the trial.
2. See if issues can be added.
3. Find at least one good issue that will be resolved in your favor.
4. Dramatize an issue or issues that form the kind of conflict you can win.
5. Determine what issues the jury can identify with.
6. Emphasize those issues during trial.
7. Deemphasize all else!

EXAMPLE: ADDING AN ISSUE DURING THE TRIAL

After listing the issues, counsel realized that another issue could be added—that is, "was his client driving fast to get away from an area where a gang of teens had been causing fights?" This is not a good defense, but it is a conflict that he can win and one he may want to interject in the story. He knows the jury by now, and he knows that each member of that jury would have been in a hurry to get away.

Counsel also knows that there was some drinking of alcohol on the part of the other driver. This is a good conflict, and although counsel may lose the question of proving intoxication, he may win the conflict of whether the drinking had some effect upon the driver. He uses the side of the conflict concerning whether or not the driver should have been drinking before driving, but avoids completely the task of proving intoxication.

CHOOSE YOUR CONFLICTS WISELY

There will be conflict in your courtroom drama. You want conflict in your courtroom drama. You do not want conflict, however, that will harm your client's cause. Therein lies one of the greatest challenges that must be faced by the trial lawyer.

Study the Likely Script of Your Courtroom Drama to Find Possible Conflicts

If there were no conflict in your lawsuit, it probably would have been settled long ago. A lawsuit is not only one large conflict, but a series of small conflicts, any one of which could determine the outcome of your courtroom drama.

You must analyze your drama and list the possible conflicts that might occur. Knowing what is going to happen makes it easier to prepare for what is to come.

EXAMPLE: ANALYZING THE CONFLICTS IN YOUR DRAMA

Counsel is retained to try a lawsuit, and the client tells his story, as counsel characterizes every possible conflict.

"I left the tavern[1] about two o'clock in the morning[2] and went to my girlfriend's home.[3] As I pulled up to a stoplight, an off-duty officer[4] riding in an unmarked car[5] pulled up along side me and shouted, "Hey, buddy, pull over." I shouted back, "What for?", and he said my state license plate had expired.[6] He waved a badge at me, so I pulled over.

When I had trouble finding my driver's license[7] he shouted "Come on, you stupid bastard, I don't have all night"[8] and I guess I cussed him back.[9] With that, he came at me as though he was going to strike me[10] so I pushed him back[11] and he must have tripped[12] because he fell. He got up, pulled out his revolver, and hit me on the head,[13] and that is all I remember.[14]

Counsel must then study each of these conflicts:

1. The word tavern may be damaging to some jurors. Inquire to see if he stopped by looking for a friend, or was there all night getting drunk. This one will not help you.

2. Some people feel that one should be home by 2:00 A.M. Did he get off work at 1:30 and stopped for one beer? Prepare the jury for this conflict.

3. The same applies to going to a girlfriend's home at 2:00 A.M. Some on the jury may be rooting for him, but many will not.

4. The off-duty officer is possibly not in uniform, and this offers some reason for not recognizing him as an officer. Officers often feel everyone recognizes their status and authority without a uniform, but the public, including jurors, do not. Here is a small conflict you can win.

5. Same applies to the unmarked car.

6. "Hey buddy, pull over" is the first real drama of conflict. It is our first indication that there may be a confrontation. Let the jury know that this came from the officer, and not from your client.

7. The jury will want to know why your client had trouble finding a driver's license. Coming from a tavern at 2:00 A.M. suggests his consumption of alcohol. To win that conflict, counsel will have to show poor lighting, sloppy billfold, or if worse comes to worse, decide it is one you are going to lose and minimize its effect by not going into it or by smothering it with evidence of brutality that is not justified, even if the man had a few drinks.

8. Calling a citizen "a stupid bastard" for not finding a driver's license immediately increases the conflict, again by the officer. Make it clear to the jury that you are winning this conflict to show your client was provoked, not to

justify anything your client did or to get the officer's job. Jurors don't like "excuses" and don't like one person to get another person fired, but when a defendant comes up with a defense they do want you to poke a hole in that defense.

9. *"I guess I cussed him back" suggests the kind of conflict counsel must investigate. He must know exactly what was said and the manner in which it was said. The client is enhancing the conflict and the jury wants to know how responsible he was for this, or whether the officer was overreacting.*

10. *The officer attempting to strike the client is the first evidence of physical force and it comes from the officer. The first contact, however, comes from the client, so it is necessary to win this conflict. It must be dramatized so the jury knows the officer was attempting to use force.*

11. *The client "pushed" the officer back. To win this conflict, it will be necessary to convince the jury that this was a defensive type of action. By the time you get to court, there may be three officers who were coming to the rescue who saw your client strike the officer three times.*

12. *Did the officer "trip" or was he hit so hard that he fell to the ground, which suggests more than a little shove. Dramatize this conflict so the jury can believe your client's story.*

13. *Make sure it was a "blow" to the head. I have heard some wild explanations as to how the butt of a revolver made contact with the head of a person being arrested. Most jurors do not want to believe an officer would take the butt of his revolver and hit a person in the head with it. Dramatize to show lack of justification and evidence of brutal force.*

14. *Is that all your client remembers? Was he "out" for a few moments, or was he unconscious from the blow and did not regain consciousness until he awoke in the hospital? Or was it that the incident happened a long time ago and he does not remember what happened after that? Helplessness is an important factor in conflict. Whenever a client becomes helpless as a result of another's conduct, this factor should be dramatized.*

Conflicts with Expert Witnesses—
Win Them or Avoid Them

Lawyers often lose battles with expert witnesses. Although a simple "No questions, Your Honor" will sometimes suffice, that should come only after careful analysis. Limiting the cross-examination of experts offers a viable alternative to waiving cross-examination. The simple formula to follow is, "How many points will I gain and how many points will I lose as a result of each phase of the cross-examination?"

Suggestion: To help avoid poor results from conflicts with experts, know what you are talking about when you cross-examine an expert. Learn something about the expert's field, the language involved, and the thinking. Use the language, explain it so the jury understands, and cross-examine the expert from a position of strength.

EXAMPLE: INTERVIEWING AN EXPERT—
WITH DRAMA

"Mr. Jones, you indicated you are an MAI, which I believe means you are a member of the institute of appraisers, is that right?"

"Yes."

"This also means that you have studied certain courses and have been interviewed by your peers, and that you know and understand the basic principles of appraising real estate?"

"Yes, that is correct."

"Much of your testimony dealt with placing a value on the property in question by using the income approach or the replacement approach, is that not correct?"

"Yes."

"But you did not use the third approach, that of comparable sales, is that right?"

"No, I explained that approach did not apply as well here."

"In fact, Mr. Jones, did you not tell the jury you could find no 'comps'?"

"Yes, I did."

"By that, you were telling this jury you could not find any sale that was comparable to the property in question?"

"Yes."

"Mr. Jones, would your opinion as to the value of that property be changed if I were to show you several very recent sales of comparable property, and that those parcels of real estate were sold for nearly twice the value you have placed on my client's property?"

"Yes. I would have to consider such evidence and perhaps adjust my opinion."

Avoid Conflicts That You Will Lose

If the big conflict of the lawsuit is one you are going to lose—*settle!* Don't expect a miracle. The jury is going to take sides on the major conflict early in the trial, and there is nothing more laborious than finishing a trial after it has been lost.

Within a lawsuit you can win, there are conflicts you will lose. Know them! Prepare for them! Avoid them! Go on to conflicts you can win!

Dramatize Conflicts That You Will Win

When you feel you can win a conflict, drain it of every possible gain you can get from it. How dare opposing counsel even raise the question of liability when we really should be talking about this woman's injuries? Don't let a witness or opposing counsel forget for one moment a conflict that you are winning. *Dramatize it!*

EXAMPLE: DRAMATIZING CONFLICT IN THE COURTROOM

In one jury trial, counsel cross-examined four expert witnesses the same day. Fortunately, three of the four were attorneys, so the "territory" was a familiar one.

"Mr. Jones, you testified you charged my client for thirteen hours of research, is that right?"

"Yes."

"And your experts have testified that the reasonable value of that time is $150 an hour, is that right?"

"Yes."

"So that research would come to $1,950?"

"Yes, I guess so."

"I assume that research was aimed at the central issue in the lawsuit that you were handling for my client, and not some other matter?"

"Why, of course."

"And that issue was the validity or invalidity of a deed that was signed in blank prior to execution?"

"Yes. That is right."

"Did you, after 13 hours of research, find a case that was in point?"

"No, there is no such case in Florida."

Counsel went back to the counsel table and picked up a lawbook and walked back to the witness stand and handed the book to the witness.

"Mr. Jones, during the lunch hour the law librarian was kind enough to lend me this book. What book have I handed you?"

"It is one of the volumes of the *Florida Digest*."

"Will you turn to the part on deeds?"

"Yes."

"Now, on the first page the first title is 'Requisites and Validity,' is that right?"

"Yes."

"Now look under B of that section, and you find a subsection on 'Form and Contents of Instruments,' do you not?"

"Yes."

"Now, under that section, look at key number 32. Does that have the word 'blanks' after it?"

"Yes."

"Now, Mr. Jones, if you will turn to key number 32 in this book under deeds, tell me if there are any decisions reported under that key number?"

"Yes. There is a case."

"*Simpson v. Hirshberg.*"

"And what is the citation to that case?"

"30 So.2d Reporter 912."

"Now, Mr. Jones, that means that this case is reported on page 912 of volume 30 of the *Southern Second* series, is that right?"

"Yes. That's what it means, Mr. Wright."

Counsel walked back to the counsel table and picked up another lawbook and approached the witness stand again.

"You know, Mr. Jones, I just happen to have that volume here in the courtroom."

The jury laughed a little. Counsel handed the book to the witness and asked him to turn to page 912.

"Now, Mr. Jones, have you found the case of *Simpson v. Hirshberg?*"

"Yes, I have."

"I find three headnotes in that case, is that what you find?"

"Yes."

"Will you read to the jury the first headnote?"

The witness paused for a moment, read it to himself, and then rather grudgingly read to the jury, "A deed which did not contain the names of grantees was void."

The witness had testified that after thirteen hours of research he could not find such a case and that, in fact, there was no such case in Florida, yet he was able to find the exact case in only a few minutes, and he did it right in front of the jury!

CONCLUSION

Conflict is tne trial lawyer's best friend and his worst enemy. Conflict gets and keeps the jury's attention! Conflict causes jurors to join your cause! Conflict win. lawsuits! However, everything conflict can do for you, it can also ao ror opposing counsel.

KEEPING CONFLICT ON YOUR SIDE

1. Emphasize conflicts you can win.
2. Minimize conflicts you may lose.
3. Show the jury you are comfortable with conflict and they will not place too much importance on conflicts you lose.

CHAPTER THIRTEEN

Study Dramatic Techniques

THE DRESS REHEARSAL
OF YOUR COURTROOM DRAMA

No actor would walk onto a stage without having rehearsed his part. No director would face an opening night crowd without having held a dress rehearsal. No trial lawyer should begin his courtroom drama without having prepared with this same professionalism.

Prepare Your Client for "Opening Night"

Some lawyers have the misconception that "rehearsal" means "manufactured" or "manipulated." Rehearsal means prepared! If you are not prepared, you should not walk into the courtroom.

You cannot, of course, have a full-blown dress rehearsal of your courtroom drama. You can, however, rehearse segments of your drama, and do it effectively. You can rehearse the closing argument within hours after you have been retained.

Rehearse that part of your final argument as you drive to and from the courthouse. That part of the argument tells the jury why you are entitled to a judgment. Rehearsing it reminds you of the theme and helps you prepare every aspect of the trial.

"Rehearse" Certain Parts of Your Drama

When you finish a deposition, you may want to start rehearsing your cross-examination of that witness. Commit to memory those few statements he or she made that will enable you to bury him or her at the trial. "Now, Mr. Jones, didn't you tell me at the deposition that you were too drunk to see the other car?"

You can rehearse parts of your *voir dire* months in advance. In every criminal case, you will want to talk about reasonable doubt, and in representing a plaintiff in a civil case, you will always want to distinguish the burden of proof from that of a criminal case.

You also should find something in your *voir dire* that will be different from your *voir dire* in other cases. Perhaps it's a weakness in your case or maybe it's a strength. Perhaps it's a criminal record or maybe it's a special way the jury can identify with your client. Mark that part of your *voir dire*, "This deserves special treatment," and rehearse it!

Your client probably has never testified in court. You not only are entitled to know what he or she is going to say, but how he or she is going to say it. If "rehearsal" sounds too much like putting words in your client's mouth, "review" his or her testimony.

Suggesting what a witness should say before asking for his testimony is to be avoided as much as the witness who asks, "What do I have to say to win?" You can avoid such trespasses and still prepare for trial.

Prepare Your Entire Cast

Talk with friendly witnesses in your office and hold your "dress rehearsal" of unfriendly witnesses at depositions. All depositions are, to some degree, a dress rehearsal. Use the deposition for that purpose! Take your cast to the courtroom in advance if that will make them more comfortable.

Study Your Stage

Feel comfortable on the stage upon which you will perform. Study it carefully. If the witness can't see the blackboard, move it a little so everyone in the courtroom can perform and help your drama move smoothly.

"Pre-Trial" Even When Pre-Trial Is Not Required

The pre-trial conference is not a rehearsal, but it is a part of trial preparation that helps accomplish the same thing. If the court rules do not require pre-trial, or if the custom does not require a thorough pre-trial, don't deny yourself of this step in your preparation. Prepare a trial brief, and prepare your trial notebook.

EXAMPLE: USING A DRESS REHEARSAL

Our Saturday morning breakfast club of mostly lawyers convened a few blocks from the St. Louis County courthouse. The film The Verdict, starring Paul Newman, had just opened at the local theaters. The movie was based on a novel by Barry Reed, a leading Boston trial lawyer, so a trial lawyer's film was about to be reviewed by a trial lawyer's severest critics, other trial lawyers.

Abe Davis, a senior member of the group, started the review by saying, "What I thought was really outstanding was the scene of the dress rehearsal conducted by the senior member of a large law firm." What was there about this scene that impressed this lawyer of many years' courtroom experience?

The doctor who was going to testify as the defendant in a medical malpractice case was sitting at the end of a huge conference room. The video camera was in operation, several members or associates of the firm sat at the conference table, and a "jury" of associates sat at the side.

The senior partner started the cross-examination, and soon the doctor said "she," and the arm of a young associate went up. The senior partner nodded as though to say "good point," and turned to the witness and shouted, "Debbie, Doctor, her name is Debbie." The doctor proceeded, being sure to call his former patient by her first name.

Soon the doctor used medical language to describe what was happening and the senior partner shouted, "She threw up in her mask, that's what she did, Doctor." The doctor is cautioned to be affirmative and to use three-word sentences.

The doctor continued his testimony and as he reached the crucial point the senior partner has to help him and suggests, ". . . and you brought thirty years' experience to bear" and the doctor agreed, and is inspired to tell how he did all that could have been done to save the girl from brain damage, and for this ending the old lawyer shouts, "Good! Good!"

They were very close to having it down right, but it had to be in the words of the doctor, because he would be alone on the stand during the courtroom drama, so the senior partner looked at the doctor and said, "Now tell us!" We knew the dress rehearsal was not over.

Dress in the Courtroom Is Important

During your dress rehearsal, give thought to your client's attire. When F. Lee Bailey addressed the Florida Bar Convention, he explained how they "dressed" Patty Hearst so she would not look like a comrad or commando. The fancy dress they had her wear would convince the jury she was a captive of the activists who held her. The famous trial lawyer said he made a mistake, however, when he handed her the machine gun, because the way she stripped the gun right in front of the jury, gave her an appearance that did not match her beautiful clothing.

CONCLUSION

A courtroom drama needs as much of a dress rehearsal as any other kind of drama. This preparation must include a preparation of your client and your witnesses, so you know what they will look and sound like, and what impression they will make. You only are entitled to one performance, so be ready for it.

THE STEPS TO A DRESS REHEARSAL

1. Confer with witnesses before trial.
2. At that conference, suggest that they dress as they are, or make suggestions as to how they may change their appearance and why.
3. Familiarize clients and witnesses with the courtroom.
4. Have witnesses present their story under courtroom conditions.

PROJECT WORDS AND EMOTIONS

Telling your story through characters who project words and emotions is an effective way to tell your story. To project means to tell your story so the audience can hear and understand.

Make Sure Your Witnesses Project

Lawyers often tell a witness, during direct or cross, to speak up. They never tell a witness to be more dramatic, or not to speak in a monotone. Such suggestions in front of the jury would not make sense, but you can give such advice before a witness takes the stand.

Witnesses must be sincere, and must sound sincere. Do nothing to make them appear to be actors and actresses. Do nothing that robs them of their freshness and genuineness. However, this does not mean that you cannot bring out this sincerity effectively. When you interview witnesses, you will find at times that they show an interest or perk up for some reason. Use those moments at the trial, by recreating those moments with questions or even "instructions" that will prompt the witness to project.

Make Sure You Project

Nothing need be said about your role. We certainly should assume you are going to project your message. Monitor you own performance, however, and see if the jurors are listening and understanding. Change the pitch of your voice, your position, and all that is necessary for your message to be transmitted.

Emphasize the "Good Things"

Make sure that the good things are heard. Alert the jurors that something good is coming. People often don't hear because they are not paying attention. Get their attention, and then keep it by talking in an interesting manner. Time the presentation of "good things."

EXAMPLE:

During direct examination, counsel said:

> "Mrs. Jones, following the collision did you talk with the other driver?"
> "Yes."
> "Where was he at the time?"
> "Sitting in his car."

"Did you notice anything unusual as you approached his car?"

"Yes. I could smell alcohol."

"Did you notice anything unusual about his appearance?"

"Yes. He appeared to have been drinking heavily."

"Which of you spoke first?"

"He did."

"Do you remember exactly what he said?"

"Yes. He said, 'I'm sorry, I didn't even see you.'"

"Your witness."

Project Nonverbally

A great deal of your communication will be without words, so make sure that you and the other characters of your drama walk, stand, sit, move their hands and arms, use their eyes, and employ all other nonverbal powers as effectively as possible. Have a witness pause for effect. If she is distressed the first time she looks at a photo, have her look distressed as she examines the photo in the courtroom.

EXAMPLE: PROJECTING EMOTIONS
TO GET THE STORY TOLD

Counsel reviewed the testimony with the witness in his office the day before the trial. "After each question I will look at the jury, and I will want you to look at the jury." He told her how to dress and how to act from the moment she arrived at the courthouse. "The woman you beat out for a parking space may be the woman who casts a vote on the jury."

When she was called as a witness, counsel helped her to the witness stand, and placed her crutches where they would not be in the way, but still within view of the jury. Twice during the examination, he asked if she needed a recess, and once said, "I know this is difficult for you, but . . ."

"Mrs. Jones, I want you to look at what has been marked Plaintiff's exhibit 1, do you recognize it?"

"Yes. It was our automobile."

"Does this picture fairly and accurately portray your automobile after the accident?"

"Yes. It does."

"Mrs. Jones, where was your husband sitting at the time of the collision?"

"On the driver's side."

"Do you know if any part of your husband's body came in contact with any part of the automobile at the time of the collision?"

"Yes."

"Mrs. Jones, I would like you to show me the part of the car that your husband's body had contact with."

"His head hit this area right here (pointing)."

"Will you please mark that area with an X?"

"Sure." Witness marks exhibit.

"Your witness."

CONCLUSION

You, and the characters you use to tell your story, must project words and emotions. Otherwise, your story will not be heard, understood, and appreciated. You have a story to tell. *Tell it!*

KEY WORDS AND EMOTIONS TO GET YOUR STORY TOLD SUCCESSFULLY

1. Use words that suggest a favorable response, such as the car "smashed" into the other car, or the officer "beat" the plaintiff, or the plaintiff "ignored" the warning.
2. Use emotions that dramatize your lawsuit, such as the loneliness of a widow who misses her deceased husband, the embarrassment of a defamatory statement, or the pain suffered from serious injury.

IN DELIVERING A MESSAGE, REMEMBER— TIMING, TIMING, AND TIMING

Attorneys rely upon timing. This simple device can add effectiveness to your performance in the courtroom.

Timing Techniques to Help You Win Cases

Timing means introducing evidence or making a statement at the right time. Timing also means delivering your story at the right pace, pausing at one moment, and proceeding rapidly at another moment.

EXAMPLES: *Here are a few ways timing can be effective:*

1. *Choose the right moment to introduce certain evidence. You have shown defendant is liable, you have shown the outrageous nature of defendant's conduct, you have shown how your client has been damaged—now show defendant's net worth. Later, argue why a substantial verdict is the only way you will discourage such outrageous conduct.*

2. *Choose the right moment to use a witness. Too weak a witness can be lost if not used properly. Use the weak witness to introduce the star witness, using him or her later may cause the jury to ignore him or her.*

3. *Choose the right moment to introduce demonstrative evidence. If a huge photo or chart will help a witness, start with it. If that exhibit can bring a dramatic climax to the witness's testimony, and he or she does not need it during his testimony, save it!*

   "Mrs. Jones, you have told us about your son who was killed in this collision, do you have a photo of him?"

   "Yes. Here's one that I have in my purse. This was his last photograph."

4. *Proceed rapidly through that which will not help you.*

   "While at your brother's, did you have anything to drink?"

   "I had one beer when I first go there."

   "How long were you there?"

   "About three hours."

   "What was the purpose of your being at his home?"

   "To help fix his car."

"And did you do that?"

"Yes, we took the engine out and fixed it, and put it back."

5. *Take time to let the good points soak in.*

"I want you to recall for a moment the testimony of Miss Jackson. Remember how she told you what she told me in the deposition. Let me read to you that one sentence." (Counsel looks at the deposition he has just taken from the counsel table) "'The car ran onto the curb and knocked the woman down without even slowing down.'"

6. *Keep an eye on the judge, the jury, and your schedule, and adjust your pace. If the judge is about to insist you proceed more rapidly, do so without warning. If the jury is listening, keep them listening. If you are about to lose the jury, do something before you lose them. Find ways to increase the pace without losing the impact of the evidence.*

"Your Honor, instead of taking time to introduce all of these photos into evidence, I think exhibit 6 really tells the whole story. I would like to have this exhibit accepted as evidence and pass it among the jurors at this time."

You can learn to time each move with the confidence of a pro, so you know when to speed things up and when to slow things down. You will be in command because you know the importance of timing.

Use Timing to Emphasize All That Is Favorable to Your Cause

There are parts of your drama that you want jurors to remember, and there are parts of your drama that you hope they didn't even hear. Emphasize or detract with time. Call attention to what is good by pausing, by repeating, by using timing to shout *Listen!* Detract from unfavorable evidence or argument by not keeping it stage center, by getting if *offstage* as soon as possible.

Add Drama with Timing

Don't hurry through a dramatic scene that will help your cause.
Don't hurry through a dramatic sentence, or a dramatic word, that
will help you win your lawsuit.
   "This patient will never work again."
   "He tried to *kill* me."

INSPIRE EMPATHY FOR YOUR
CHARACTERS AND CAUSES

"Empathy" is a playwright's word that should mean much to the
trial lawyer. It describes a very special relationship between the
jury and witnesses or parties. Empathy can win or lose a lawsuit.

Discover How to Use Empathy in the Courtroom

The American Heritage Dictionary of English Usage defines "empathy" as "understanding so intimate that the feelings, thoughts,
and motives of one are readily comprehended by the other." The jury
must understand your cause and your characters. Your client's
feelings, thoughts, and motives must be readily comprehended. If
jurors feel close to a person or a cause, they are likely to vote for that
person or cause.

EXAMPLES: *The trial lawyer must use empathy in his or her
courtroom drama.*

1. *The jury must understand the attorney's client and the
   client's cause.*

      "My client is a 60-year-old man who had worked
      for this company for thirty years, and he was able to do
      his work better than the 30-year-old who was given my
      client's job."

2. *The jury must feel an intimate relationship with the lawyer's
   client.*

"If they can do this to Johnny Brown, they can do this to any ten-year-old boy, and then no one's son is safe in this county."

3. *The jury must know your client's feelings.*

"How do you think Mrs. Smith felt when she picked up the newspaper and read this article, knowing the whole world would think she had committed a crime, when in truth she had done no such thing?"

4. *The jury must know your client's thoughts.*

"John told you why he went there. You and I know he should not have gone there, but this young man wanted to visit this young lady. At that moment, he thought that was the most important thing in the world."

5. *The jury must understand your client's motives.*

"We don't know why Bill carried that knife. He told us he had to in that neighborhood, and there has been no evidence in this trial to show any other motive . . ."

Your client and his or her cause will be closely identified, and one may suffer from the other, but they *are* separate factors, and must be considered as such. The trial lawyer has a dual challenge, to sell his or her client and his or her cause. A jury will like a character for many abstract reasons, but it will like a cause only if that cause appeals to common sense. Remember that the jury must understand the feelings, thoughts, and motives.

Recognize Empathy as a Factor in Settlement

Long before you reach the courtroom, you must consider the empathy factor. Nothing is more important when appraising your lawsuit for the purpose of negotiating a settlement. If your theory is clearly correct but will not impress a jury or if you feel the jury just

isn't going to like your client, you had better get that settlement
brochure in the mail immediately.

Use Empathy in Your Drama to Win

Once you understand and appreciate empathy, use it! Use it in your
voir dire. If you represent a Patty Hearst or a Dr. Sam Shepard,
introduce that character in the questions you ask. Find out which
prospective jurors will have empathy for such a character.

Use it in your opening statement. You are telling the jury what
this case is all about. "This man will never again be able to play ball
with his son," or "This truck driver was driving the truck at a speed
of twenty miles an hour over the speed limit." You may get empathy
from those who feel a father should be able to play with his son, or
from those who have had a truck fly by them out on the highway.

Obtain empathy not only for your client, but for your leading
witnesses. If the jurors like a witness, they are more apt to believe
that witness.

"Mrs. Smith, you were a witness to this accident, were
you not?"

"Yes."

"And I believe you lost your son in an accident less
than a year ago?"

"That's right."

Let opposing counsel object, if he so chooses.

"Now, I have to ask you a few questions about this
accident in which my client was injured."

"Like I told the officer, I saw the whole thing and I
think it is my duty to explain what happened."

*If there is empathy in your drama, final argument must show it.
Empathy equal emotional appeal. Final argument must include an
emotional appeal.*

*It is a trial lawyer's duty to encourage empathy for his or her
client, and to find ways in which the jury will feel empathy. Know
your client! Find what about him or her will attract the jury.*

Encourage empathy in your voir dire.

"Have any of you ever been involved in a fire, one that burned your home and everything in it?"

Encourage empathy in your opening statement.

"We all love our home, and under our constitution have a right to feel secure in our home. This man was sitting in his home with his family when two police officers came and knocked on his door. These police officers took this man from his home, in front of his family, and for one reason. This big corporation *thought* this man was the person who stole something from its store."

Encourage empathy in presenting your testimony.

"How much education do you have, Mrs. Smith?"
"Eighth grade."
"Did you read this contract before signing it?"
"He said I didn't have to."
"Did he tell you what was in it?"
"Yes, he said I could pay for it anytime I was able."
"Did you believe that?"
"Yes, I trusted him."
"Tell me, Mrs. Smith, why didn't you read the contract?"
"I wouldn't understand it, anyway. I didn't want to tell anyone, but I'm not good at readin."

Encourage empathy in your final argument.

"Bill Brown has sat at this table and listened to this trial, knowing that your decision could send him to prison. Can you imagine how that must feel, and can you imagine what he has been thinking? We will never know exactly what happened in that tavern that night, but we know that there is no evidence upon which this young man can be convicted. Yet, he sits here, awaiting your verdict. I trust

that your verdict will be a verdict of not guilty, because
under the law of our state and under the evidence of this
case this man is simply not guilty. He has suffered enough.
Send him home where he belongs."

EXAMPLE: GETTING THE JURY TO EMPATHIZE WITH YOUR CLIENT

*The trial lawyer must (a) cause the jury to like his client, and (b)
give the jury reason to find in his client's favor. Counsel accomplished both by appealing to the human emotions of the
jurors:*

"Mrs. Jones, how long did your mother live in the
nursing home?"

"About three years."

"Did you visit her on April 13, 1983?"

"Yes."

"What happened when you arrived at the nursing
home on that day?"

"The manager met me at the door and rushed me into
his office. He explained that my mother nearly fell out of
bed, that the nurse caught her, just in time."

"Was she injured?"

"No, not on that occasion."

"Did you discuss this incident with the manager?"

"Yes. I told him that they should never leave my
mother unattended. If it takes extra money for this service,
let me know."

"What was his response?"

"He assured me that there would never be a moment
when my mother was not attended."

"Did you go to that home on June 2, of that same year?"

"Yes."

"What happened when you arrived at the home on that
day?"

"I saw a nurse running to my mother's room, so I ran to
the room also."

"What did you find when you arrived at the room?"

"My mother was on the floor, screaming in pain."

"What did you do?"

"I told them to get an ambulance, immediately, and take my mother to a hospital."

"Was anyone in the room besides your mother, and the nurse who had just run into the room, when you arrived?"

"No, there was no one else."

"Mrs. Jones, were you in the courtroom this morning when this lady at the table here told the jury it was your mother's own fault that she fell?"

"Yes, I was."

"Had you requested that your mother be transferred to one of the cottages?"

"Yes, I did."

"Mrs. Jones, let me show you what has been marked as plaintiff's exhibit number 6. Do you recognize this piece of paper?"

"Yes. It is a letter I received from the nursing home."

"Would you please read it to the jury."

"Sure. 'Dear Mrs. Jones. I am sorry, but your mother cannot be transferred to a cottage because she needs the constant care available only in the main facility. She is often disoriented. She is a very proud person and tries to do more than she is capable of doing. She is a joy to have with us, always trying to cheer up the others, but she has to have someone look after her every minute.'"

When you are seeking empathy, you must reach down and grab at the emotions of the jury.

"Today there are many people who don't want to work. Mary Smith wants to work, but she will never be able to work again. She wants to take care of her children, but she cannot do today what she did before the accident. You heard her testimony about the picnic last summer. Her children called her to come and play with them, but she could not play with them. Mary Smith will never be able to play with her children again."

No, not a Lenny or a Willy Loman, just another person who ends up as a leading character in a courtroom drama. He or she is a person who needs to be understood by the jury. It is your job to accomplish that!

CONCLUSION

The trial lawyer has a duty to help the jury understand so intimately the feelings, thoughts, and motives of the characters of his or her courtroom drama. That is empathy—that is what will help you win your lawsuit!

HOW TO GET A JURY TO EMPATHIZE

1. Personalize your client and you will humanize him or her.
2. Appeal to the jury by sharing your client's thoughts with them.
3. Tell the jury why your client did what he or she did, even if it was wrong.

CHAPTER FOURTEEN

Bring Drama into the Courtroom

HOW TO MAKE COURTROOM DRAMA HAPPEN

For centuries, the drama of a murder trial has been overly appreciated, and the drama of other trials has been under-appreciated. Most lawsuits don't sound exciting to the layman. That is the challenge facing you the trial lawyer as you prepare your courtroom drama.

If we do not tell our story in an interesting manner, if we do not bring drama into the courtroom, we have missed our objective. Drama is a necessary part of the courtroom scene, but it doesn't just happen. You have to create it!

EXAMPLE: DRAMATIZING
CROSS-EXAMINATION

Counsel could have asked one question, but made the cross-examination more dramatic by asking three questions:

"Mr. Smith, did you tell the court at preliminary hearing that you were in the room at the time the alleged crime was committed?"

"Yes."

"Did you tell me at your deposition that you were in the room at the time the alleged crime was committed?"

"Yes."

"Mr. Smith, I want to ask you . . . and I remind you that you are under oath . . . are you telling this jury today that you were *not* in the room?"

Recognize the Fact that Courtroom Drama
Must Be Planned

Find the courtroom style that makes you feel most comfortable and use that style to plan your courtroom drama. Don't imitate others, but study others, and find out what it takes to be a trial lawyer who can walk into a courtroom and properly present his or her courtroom drama.

You may have to be tougher in the courtroom, and in negotiations and all else that leads to the courtroom than you are in ordinary life.

It is most important for you to understand your ego, and the ego of others, and to use this understanding to your advantage.

EXAMPLE: *Counsel rose and walked toward the jury box. He spoke slowly and logically. He made no attempt to outshout opposing counsel. He was so deliberate in his speech that he could see the jury follow his argument step by step.*

He was tempted to be very clever by embarrassing a witness. This would make him appear to be a smart lawyer, and satisfy his ego, but he realized it might also cause the jury to sympathize with the witness. It was his style to proceed in a very quiet and logical manner, and that is what he did.

Use Drama for One Reason—To Win!

Your ego should serve to make you a better trial lawyer, to prompt you to do all that is within your capability, to imagine beyond your capability. Drama should serve but one purpose in the courtroom—to win!

EXAMPLE: *The insurance company had made a substantial offer, but the lawyer saw an opportunity to obtain one of the largest verdicts ever obtained in that county. This lawyer hid from his client the fact the offer had been made and ignored advice from lawyers associated with him to settle the case.*

This lawyer gave a dramatic final argument, but the jury decided against his client. That final argument was not given for the purpose of winning the case, since he had already gotten as good an offer as his verdict could reasonably have been. The final argument

*was to satisfy this lawyer's ego, and caused him to become a
defendant in a malpractice suit.*

If you ever confuse the two, and use drama to satisfy your own
ego, you are going to be in big trouble.

Without drama, a trial is sterile and boring. Without drama, you
are forfeiting your most effective weapon. Make drama happen and
it will help you win. Plan drama, as you plan every other aspect of
your trial.

EXAMPLE: INNOVATING TO CREATE DRAMA

*Counsel had tried just about every kind of lawsuit, and then one day
he appeared before the Arbitration Committee of the New York
Stock Exchange. The hearing is conducted by a Wall Street lawyer
before three experts in the field of securities and investments. The
hearing was held within the oak-panelled walls of the old Missouri
Athletic Club.*

> When the afternoon session began, counsel rose and
> said: "This morning I indicated the plaintiff had no further
> evidence, but I would like to reopen plaintiff's case for the
> sole purpose of reading into evidence one document."
>
> "Permission granted."
>
> "During the lunch hour my client and I had lunch at
> the Polynesian Restaurant across the street. When she
> opened her fortune cookie, it read, 'Your money will be
> returned to you many times over.' I would like to file this as
> an exhibit for the plaintiff."

*Starting the afternoon session that way relaxed the stuffy
atmosphere and set the stage for a gruelling cross-examination of an
executive of a Los Angeles brokerage firm. The verdict reestablished
counsel's faith in fortune cookies.*

What does this have to do with being a trial lawyer? EVERY-
THING!!

A willingness to do something different, a willingness to
experiment, and a feeling of being at home wherever there is conflict
is very much a part of being a trial lawyer. Melvin Belli is credited
with many innovations, such as demonstrative evidence, but his

greatest contribution to the trial bar is telling trial lawyers, "You are not a good trial lawyer unless you can walk into any courtroom anywhere in the country and try any kind of a lawsuit."

At a trial lawyers conference, I sat at the same table with Jack Fuchsberg and listened to him tell of that first million dollar verdict. The judge was going to have him removed from representing the minor because he wouldn't accept a settlement of half what he eventually got from the jury. The pressure on a lawyer in such a case is beyond imagination. It takes "guts" to be a good trial lawyer.

CONCLUSION

Bring drama to the courtroom! Don't expect it to just happen. MAKE IT HAPPEN! Use drama effectively, and you will win!

KEYS TO EFFECTIVE COURTROOM DRAMA

1. Be willing to dramatize.
2. Don't think you are going to create drama, you must recognize drama in the real world and bring it into the courtroom.
3. Make sure your drama is sincere and believable.
4. Time your drama so it is effective.

HOW TO USE HUMAN EMOTIONS

1. Evaluate your lawsuit from the outset on the basis of human emotion, or jury appeal.
2. Look for emotional appeal, or lack of appeal, in your client.
3. During deposition, watch the witness closely, and size up the witness for appeal to emotion.
4. During *voir dire* watch for what part of the lawsuit seems to spark an emotional response on the part of prospective jurors.
5. Direct oral testimony and demonstrative evidence toward those aspects of your lawsuit which have emotional appeal.
6. Leave certain moments of the trial stage center to draw as much emotional appeal as possible.

EVALUATE HUMAN EMOTION— THE HIDDEN WEAPON THAT HAS SUNK LAWYERS FOR CENTURIES

The law you learn in law school is important and the appellate court decisions you read each day will help keep you apprised, but winning or losing lawsuits often depends upon those abstract factors you learn only in the courtroom. You must learn how to deal with the human emotions that surface during your courtroom drama.

EXAMPLE: *The question was whether or not the defendant stole some food from a supermarket. The evidence was clear that she was guilty. The fact that her husband had been out of work and her welfare check was late due to red tape had nothing to do with her innocence or guilt. Counsel raised technical defenses and with it dramatically put before the court the plight of the defendant. The ruling on the technicality could have gone either way, but went the way of the defendant, because a trial lawyer recognized the human emotion factor, and used it dramatically.*

Understand Human Emotions

When a client tells me that he or she has a right to certain relief, I tell myself, and sometimes my client, the judge and jury have the right to decide against this client, if there is sufficient evidence to sustain such a conclusion. Rights, laws and legal remedies are but the framework within which a conclusion is reached. It is usually the human emotion factor that prevails, especially where other factors are equal, or at least not overpowering.

EXAMPLE: *It was the officer's word against that of the defendant. The burden of proof beyond a reasonable doubt was one that usually would cause the prosecution much concern. The defendant, however, dressed flamboyantly, was an arrogant witness, refused to answer certain questions for no apparent reason, and challenged the Court to decide against him. The court accepted that challenge!*

Select Jurors Who Will Respond
to the Human Appeal of Your Drama

In selecting a jury, you must remember that jurors react similarly to hard, cold facts, but one juror reacts much differently from another when evaluating the emotional issues of a lawsuit. That is why you must evaluate the emotional issues of your case before deciding on a judge or jury, or one prospective juror over another.

EXAMPLE: *Here are a few emotional issues that may be hiding in a lawsuit:*

1. *Some female jurors are jealous of female plaintiffs.*
2. *Fear of crime may cause a prospective juror to hide his or her true feelings during voir dire.*
3. *Racial or religious feelings may cause a juror to vote against a person, or to lean too far the other way, trying to be fair.*
4. *Picturing one of the parties as a close friend or relative may cause the juror to lean toward that person.*
5. *Not wanting others to have more money than the juror has may cause that juror to vote against a large verdict, though the large verdict is warranted by the evidence.*
6. *Wanting to conform to what other jurors are saying is often a factor.*
7. *Feeling toward counsel is often as important, as feeling toward counsel's client.*
8. *Jurors simply return better verdicts for people they like.*

In negotiating a lawsuit, don't ignore the emotional factor. It has a big dollar value as a plus or minus, so you simply cannot evaluate your case without giving serious, honest, and intelligent consideration to this factor.

Control Human Emotions
That Might Hurt You

Don't let the state introduce a bloody photo of the victim when a less emotional photo will tell the same story. During *voir dire*, have prospective jurors tell you they will not be influenced by sympathy. During final argument, ask them to follow the oath they have given.

If an emotional scene will help opposing counsel, get it over early in the trial. If opposing counsel tried to drag it on, show the jury what he or she is doing and suggest that is all there is to his or her side of the case.

Determine What Parts of Your Drama Will Involve Human Emotion

Lawyers always talk about the three requirements of a good lawsuit, liability, damages, and collectibility. They are all "musts," but I also talk about that fourth factor, *jury appeal.* "Will the jury get excited about this lawsuit?" That may well depend upon the human emotions factor.

Don't assume that all people have a warm, emotional feeling for other human beings. There are judges and jurors who do not, so beware. You must obtain the best jury you can and present your human issues as effectively as possible.

Display Your Presentation of the Human Emotions of Your Drama with Honesty

There is nothing that hurts a trial lawyer more than for the jury to think he is just putting on a show. His credibility depends upon his drama being presented with honesty and sincerity.

EXAMPLE: *If you talk about the "poor defendant" you will cause the jury to wonder about the "poor victim." Telling the jury to send this boy home to his mother, with all the tears you can muster, will sound hollow unless you have shown the jury why he should go home.*

If you can convince the jury an officer struck your client, this proof itself will be dramatic, if presented with the drama it deserves. Asking the jury to believe you because you are shouting the accusation dramatically will not suffice.

If a lawyer proves his or her eyewitness is a prostitute and asks the jury to disbelieve her solely for that reason, the jurors may stare at the lawyer as if to say, "What does this possibly have to do with the lawsuit?" If, however, the lawyer emphasizes a flaw in her testimony, the jury may definitely consider the source from which the testimony came.

Presenting evidence dramatically entitles counsel to talk about it more dramatically. Let the plaintiff tell why she could not play with her children, and then during final argument a mere reference to that scene will bring an emotional response.

EXAMPLE: UNDERSTANDING HUMAN EMOTIONS

We trial lawyers sometimes feel God is on our side when the emotional issues are on our side. This has led to many disappointments. You sometimes wonder how a judge could send this young man to prison, how a trial judge could take a child from a deserving father, or how an appellate court could take half a million dollars from an injured person because of a technicality that had nothing to do with the outcome of the trial.

Counsel represented a woman who was sueing her son to collect money she had lent him. The mother was now destitute and the son showed an obnoxious lack of concern for his mother and his obligation to her.

The mother's case had tons of "jury appeal," but a legal technicality stood between her and justice. Opposing counsel pushed for a court ruling on a statue of limitations question that would have sent the mother out the courtroom door without a dime.

The judge called a recess, and met with the attorneys in chambers to argue the motion. The young lawyer representing the son argued the law, and the mother's attorney countered with the best argument he could muster.

The judge heard all argument, then paused for a few minutes, then looked up at the son's attorney and said, "You have offered some good argument, but I am going to rule against you."

"Why, Judge, why?" the young lawyer shouted, "There is no basis for your ruling, Judge, why are you deciding against me?"

The judge looked up and in a very plain and clear language that anyone could understand, said simply, "Because your client is an asshole."

You may never have heard of this rule of law. Blackstone did not comment on it in his *Commentaries*. Holmes did not mention it in his *Common Law*. Neither the Napoleonic code, nor any other code, contains a provision relating to it, but it is a rule of law. In one form or other, it has been with us for years, guiding judges and jurors, and surprising the hell out of young attorneys. It is the unwritten law guided by human emotions.

The woman got her judgment and was saved from all that was evil and wrong.

CONCLUSION

Without human emotion, there would be no drama in the courtroom. Emotion is the "stuff" of which drama is made. Emotional involvement is not enough alone to win a lawsuit, but without it your drama has a hard time taking off. Understand emotions and use them to help you win your lawsuit.

HOW TO BETTER UNDERSTAND EMOTIONS

1. Look for factors that may cause a person to compromise with reason.
2. Recognize that this compromise may be knowingly, such as voting to convict though the juror knows there is a reasonable doubt, or unknowingly where the juror convinces himself or herself that the verdict is right, though unable to explain it with reason.
3. Recognize that emotion may not be a factor in the decision, but in the degree of action taken once the decision is made, such as a reasonable decision that the defendant was wrong but an unreasonable *size of* verdict because the juror felt sorry for the plaintiff.
4. Recognize that emotion may cause bias toward a party, or prejudice against a party, with equal force.
5. Examine your own emotions, and understand why you have strong feelings on certain subjects.
6. Emotion can be perceived as a wonderful, warm characteristic, or as a betrayal of trust, a poor substitute for the reasoning process guaranteed by the constitution.
7. Treat with special care this human characteristic, never degrading it, but when it works against your client, explaining and even sympathizing with the position, but reminding jurors of the necessity of deciding cases upon their merits.

ACCEPT YOUR CHALLENGE—
EXPLAIN ONE HUMAN BEING TO ANOTHER

It is the task of the trial lawyer to explain one human to another. How well you explain will determine the outcome of your courtroom drama.

Know Your Client

You must interview your client. You must see him or her in action at a deposition. You must interrogate him or her at length to get his or her reaction to what will happen at trial.

Others can furnish you with information, but you must be familiar with that information. You must understand your characters with thoroughness.

EXAMPLES: *Avoid the unexpected by asking such questions:*

1. *Questions relating to the incident ("Why are you sure the light was red?")*
2. *Questions that tell you about your client and his background ("What other jobs have you had?")*
3. *Questions touching on what you feel will be your strongest points ("Describe the other driver's appearance?")*
4. *Questions touching on what you feel will be your weakest points ("Tell me everything you did since leaving prison.")*
5. *Questions relating to subjects you feel will stir the emotions of the jury ("Tell me, in detail, how you felt when you saw your husband.")*
6. *Questions that may suggest the use of demonstrative evidence or real evidence ("Do you have any photos of your son?")*

Some clients really don't impress us, but they are the clients that need our special attention. With them, we must try a little harder to find that image we want to project.

We have all met people who did not impress us at first meeting, because of their physical appearance. Once we got to know them, we liked them. Some clients require more time for the jury to know them and understand them. Plan your drama to include that time.

Know What About Your Client Can Help Win

There is good and bad in every client, and in every witness. It is your job to accentuate the positive. Look for it, because it is there. Once you find it, *exploit it!*

Some clients need a lot of explaining. Why would someone do what they did? There *is* a reason. Find it! People are not perfect, and sometimes jurors appreciate imperfection.

Present Your Client's Image to the Jury

Present your characters honestly! Jurors can forgive a lot, but they just don't forgive easily someone who has not been honest with them. If your client has a weakness, that will come out at the trial. Mention it first, get credit for being honest. If that weakness isn't supposed to come out at trial, under the rules of evidence, make sure it doesn't reach the jury. File your motion in limine!

The jurors want to know about your client. In a criminal case, the jurors want to know what he or she did and why he or she did it. They want you to explain your client.

Have your client testify, if at all possible. Have him or her testify in person, and not by deposition, if at all possible. If he or she must testify by deposition, make it a video deposition. At all times when he or she is in the courtroom, make sure he or she gives the proper image.

EXAMPLE: *The client has been injured in an accident. If she still uses crutches, she uses them going to and from the courtroom. She dresses as though she is going to court, even if she normally wears blue jeans to work. This is a serious matter, so she is not joking during recess. She does not use words she does not understand, but she tells her story intelligently. She has reviewed her depositions so she knows how to answer questions covered in it. She has had a conference with her attorney and has even visited the courtroom so she feels comfortable on the witness stand. She looks at the jurors while testifying, as though conversing with them.*

Let others tell his or her story, also. You tell his or her story, during *voir dire*, opening statement, and final argument. Explain your client with demonstrative evidence.

EXAMPLE: *The client testified that following the first operation she complained of pain in the groin. In addition to this testimony, her attorney introduced a positive X-ray showing the clamp that had been left in her body following the first operation. From this exhibit the jury knew one thing about the plaintiff—she had good reason to complain.*

Practice Explaining People to People

When our family was travelling on vacation a news report came over the radio that a little boy was lost. Ed was very young at the time, and he said, "Why don't we try to help find that little boy, his parents must be very worried." This is all you need to know about my oldest son. You now know of what he is made. Whether he made an error at shortstop or hit in the winning run is not important. I have already explained a warm human being, and it only took me two sentences in which to do it.

Other people are harder to explain. Several years ago, St. Louis County was shocked by a series of rapes. When the "animal," as he was called by the press, was captured, he told the deputy sheriff, "I had 250 women in this county, and only six of them complained." What does that tell you about this man? Are you more convinced he is an "animal"? Does it disgust you that he can joke about such horrible crimes? Beware of a sense of humor, even at most inappropriate times.

My wife occasionally suggests a case that might convince me this man should be executed, if ever there is a need for capital punishment. How could I respond when she describes the brutal killing of nine people by a man who had no remorse for what he had done? I took the matter under advisement and gave my reply a few months later, after a chance meeting with the man's cellmate.

The man had been in prison, prior to the murders, and every night the guard would walk by, and due to a physical handicap the man could not close his eyes while sleeping. The guard, several times a night, would hit the man with his stick and shout, "Don't look at me you no good bastard." That is how the man had spent his entire life, because of a simple handicap.

EXAMPLE: EXPOSING THE WRONGS
OF YOUR OPPOSITION

If you are going to crucify a witness, prepare for this dramatic event with thoroughness. A popular radio station conducted a "treasure hunt," in which clues were given periodically, and finally 12,000 people were looking frantically throughout St. Louis for a capsule containing the winning certificate. There was one problem, up to the last day there was no capsule hidden, so 12,000 people were looking for something that wasn't there.

Counsel represented one of those 12,000 people, one that came very close to winning. Counsel's job was to explain that this well-known old radio station was making fools of 12,000 people who were looking in vain. He did this through a deposition, with the aid of a bit of information as to when the capsule was actually hidden.

"Mr. _____, who was responsible for the placing of the capsule?"

"I was."

"Did you personally place the capsule at the place where it was found?"

"No. I had someone do that for me."

"How many capsules were placed during the contest?"

"One."

"Do you mean the capsule that was found the day you awarded the prize was the same one that was hidden the first day of the contest?" He became a little suspicious.

"Oh, I see what you mean. There was only one capsule hidden at a time. It may have been a different capsule."

"Was there a time when no capsule was hidden, when the people were looking for something that wasn't there?"

"No. Absolutely not."

"How many different capsules were used during the contest?"

"There were two."

"Not more than two?"

"No. Just two."

"When was the first capsule hidden?"

"Right before we began the contest."

"When was the second capsule hidden?"

"About five days before the contest ended."

"Did the second capsule replace the first one immediately?"

"Yes. The man took away the first capsule and hid the second capsule in exactly the same place immediately."

"Why was it necessary to replace the first capsule?"

"Because of the weather."

"What affect did the weather have on the capsule?"

"It created moisture in the capsule, and we were afraid the winning certificate would be damaged."

"And what caused that moisture?"

"Rain."

"Mr. _____, let me show you what I have marked plaintiff's exhibit 1. Do you recognize this?"

"I have not seen it before."

"This is a weather report from the United States Weather Bureau giving the official weather conditions for this area during the entire period of the contest. Can you find any day, or any hour, during that period in which it rained?"

He could not. The client received a settlement larger than the prize money, but the case did not end there. About a year later, an attorney for the FCC asked to borrow a copy of the deposition. Within a matter of months, the radio station lost its license, stockholders lost money, and employees lost their jobs. All because of a little deposition that explained what one human being did to 12,000 other human beings.

This is one of the trial lawyer's toughest challenges, explaining what a person in authority of a large well-known company did to other human beings. People just don't want to believe that people are that way.

It took an explosively written memorandum in the Ford Pinto automobile case to convince a jury that Ford Motor Company knew people may be barbecued in their little automobile, but correcting the cause of this would be too costly. It took similar discovery in the Dalkon Shield cases to show that the sales people for the company were warned not to let doctors know that the product might cause cancer.

Lawyers in the criminal practice live with this problem every day. Jurors come from a law-and-order society that assumes police officers do not lie. During the Watergate scandal, when the director of the FBI admitted to destroying evidence, the image of the FBI remained intact, and today people just don't believe some of the practices of all police officers.

CONCLUSION

You must explain to the jury the weaknesses and even the intentional wrongs committed by those who have harmed your clients. You must explain the weaknesses and even the wrongs of your own client. First, however, you must understand what makes people function as human beings, and you must explain this to the jury. The jury will be looking for simple answers, and you must explain the interworkings of the complex machinery we call a human being.

HOW TO DISCREDIT WHEN YOU CROSS EXAMINE

1. Determine how aggressive you should be to minimize the discrediting, while minimizing the jury sympathy for the witness.
2. Show bias, reasons the witness favors the other side.
3. Show prejudice, reasons the witness testified against your client.
4. Show incorrectness, the lack of reliability.
5. Use drama, by being subtle or direct, as the situation requires.

MOTIVATE—OR LOSE

Clarence Darrow said people don't want to send other people to prison, and you have to give them a reason not to. In every kind of lawsuit, you, as the trial lawyer, have to inspire the jury to do what you feel they must do. You must *MOTIVATE OR LOSE!*

Find the Part of Your Story That Will Inspire the Jury

You are required to plead and prove what will constitute the theory of your case. When you have a choice, choose the one that will impress the jury. Once you choose your theory, tell the jury the part of the story that will impress them most.

EXAMPLE: *When the prosecutor finished his opening statement, defense counsel rose and told the jury:*

> "The State told you about one knife, but failed to tell you about the other knife. Without this second knife there would have been no fight and no one would have been killed.
> "Our evidence will show that my client did nothing until the other young man pulled a knife and attacked him. Our evidence will show that everything my client did was in defense of his own life."

You must motivate the jury. They have not lived with this lawsuit for the past year. They do not receive one-third of the amount of the verdict. They have never met your client and will probably never see your client again.

Why should they return a verdict for your client? What difference does it really make to them? How can you convince the jury as to how important your client's cause is to your client, and to every other person who might end up in the same set of circumstances?

You can do this by:

1. Showing effect on your client ("You and I will now go home, but if you find this man guilty, he will never go home, not as the same man you send to prison").
2. Showing the effect the verdict will have on others ("What difference does it really make to this huge corporation, if it has to pay the small sum it was obligated to pay under the contract?").

3. Showing why they are doing the right thing by returning a verdict for your client ("Through your verdict you can send out the word that we are not going to tolerate the unlawful conduct committed by this man against my client").

4. Showing how this verdict may affect others ("If you find for this police officer, you are telling all police officers that once they have a gun and badge, they can do what they want").

People *are* concerned about people *when motivated*. They sit in a courtroom and within a minute can love your client and hate anyone who gets in the way of that client. By the end of a courtroom drama, law-abiding people can be cheering for a "criminal" even though the crime is contrary to law. *This is motivation!*

To *motivate people* is to *move people*. This means you must move them from their normal state of lethargy, from their unwillingness to get involved with the affairs of others, from their security blanket under which they hide from the complexities of a fast-changing world.

Look at your lawsuit and find out what about it is going to motivate the judge or jury. The bad man looks rather macho as he rides into town on a beautiful horse, but his image deteriorates dramatically as he slaps a woman, or humiliates an old man by spitting in his face. Is there a "slapping a woman" or a "spitting at an old man" scene that can be worked into your courtroom drama?

Did the old man who drove into your client complain that his smashed Cadillac was nearly new? Did the doctor who goofed in the operating room complain that he was late for an appointment on the golf course? Did the manufacturing company that caused devastating injuries have a memo in its files in which knowledge of the fault is admitted, but correcting the fault would mean lower dividends for its wealthy stockholders?

You Must Emphasize the Part of Your Story That Motivates

Somewhere in your lawsuit may be a potential scene that will motivate. Your discovery should be aimed at discovering such a scene. Your opening statement should announce the coming of such an event. Your introduction of that evidence should highlight the motivation with dramatic impact. Your final argument should remind, explain and motivate.

You Must Find Which Characters Will Most Dramatically Tell Your Story

Motivate the jury with the characters of your drama who will most effectively provide that motivation. Don't have your hero tell about the bad man spitting in the old man's face. Show this to the jury. Read his deposition or put him on the stand. "I was in a hurry to play golf" is more effective than "he was in a hurry to play golf."

Present Your Evidence with Drama

If there is a piece of paper that is going to motivate the jury, build your scene around that piece of paper. Have it fully identified and fully authenticated. Let the jury know that what they are about to see is going to blow this lawsuit wide open. Then decide whether leaving it in view will give it further persuasive power, or whether you should reverently remove it from view.

Use Your Role as the Trial Lawyer to Motivate

During *voir dire*, you must begin motivating the jury by telling prospective jurors, through all you do and say, that you must win and they can believe the story you are about to tell. During opening statement, you are still all the jury knows about your lawsuit.

Before you have put a single witness on the witness stand you have begun motivating the jury with your drama. That must continue to those final five minutes of your final argument, when you stand alone before the jury and the climax of your drama motivates the jury to return a verdict for your client.

EXAMPLE: MOTIVATING THE JURY TO FIND FOR YOUR CLIENT

"In my opening statement, I explained what our evidence would be, and we have now heard all of the evidence we will ever hear in this lawsuit. We have also heard the judge's instructions as to the law that must be applied to this evidence. My client is entitled to a judgment not only for actual damages, but for punitive damages as well.

"We now know that what John Harrison did was wrong and he knew it was wrong when he did it. We now know that what this man did was unlawful and he knew it was unlawful when he did it. We also know that under the law of this state, since what he did was wrongful and unlawful, and that he did it intentionally, you may assess punitive damages, in addition to any actual damages.

"How do you arrive at the amount of punitive damages that should be assessed? The judge has told you in his instructions that you can consider such amount as, you feel will punish this man, such amount as will deter this man, and others, from ever doing this kind of thing again.

"It takes a much larger verdict to discourage one person from repeating this kind of wrongful and unlawful conduct than it would for another person. That is why it is important that you consider the wealth of the defendant. That is why we introduced evidence as to his wealth, and that is why the judge admitted that information into evidence.

"I know you are concerned about what this man did, about the way he treated this woman I represent. We are all concerned when one human being treats another human being that way. We now know how much this woman has suffered and we now know that if this man paid for that suffering and nothing more, he would laugh at this woman, at the court, and at you and me, and would just write her a check and walk out of this courtroom.

"But, you have it within your power to do something about it. When we read in the newspaper about a terrible thing that happened we wish we could do something about it. This government of ours, with all its faults, is still the best government in the world, and this system we operate under is still the best system in the world.

"We *want* to make this system work, but it can't work if we let people push other people around, just because they have a lot of money. Most people never have an opportunity to really make our system work, but today you have such an opportunity. Today is the only day in your life that you can really do something about it.

"You can send the word out that here in America everyone must follow the same law regardless of how much money they have. You can send the word out that here in America you just don't shove someone around, regardless of how much money you have.

"How much of a verdict will it take to teach a lesson to a man who has 100 billion dollars, a man who spent one million dollars last year furnishing his plush condominium in Palm Beach? I suggest to you that you cannot punish this man, you cannot teach him and others like him that he cannot treat people the way he treated this woman, unless you return a verdict of one billion dollars."

The first eight paragraphs of that final argument came from final arguments actually given to juries. The last paragraph is from that mythical case we all expect to walk into the front door of our law office someday.

CONCLUSION

You may or may not have something to do with whether or not that big case comes walking into your office. I have not addressed that problem, and the answer is not within my expertise. I have shared with you dramatic techniques that will motivate jurors. You are now ready to obtain that billion dollar verdict!

Index